The
Oklahoma
Story

Arrell M. Gibson

The Oklahoma Story

UNIVERSITY OF OKLAHOMA PRESS
Norman

By Arrell Morgan Gibson
Published by the University of Oklahoma Press

The Kickapoos: Lords of the Middle Border (1963)

The Life and Death of Colonel Albert Jennings Fountain (1965)

Fort Smith: Little Gibraltar on the Arkansas (with Edwin C. Bearss) (1969)

The Chickasaws (1971)

Wilderness Bonanza: The Tri-State District of Missouri, Kansas, and Oklahoma (1972)

(editor) *Frontier Historian: The Life and Work of Edward Everett Dale* (1975)

The Oklahoma Story (1978)

Library of Congress Cataloging in Publication Data

Gibson, Arrell Morgan.
    The Oklahoma story.

    Includes index.
    1. Oklahoma—History.   I. Title.
F694.G523   976.6   77–18608

Dedicated to

ALECIA BETH GIBSON

a young learner

Preface

You are about to begin an adventure in reading. Through these pages you will be a witness to the excitement of *The Oklahoma Story*. It begins with our first settlers entering this land over 15,000 years ago, living in caves and hunting the Columbian mammoth and other huge animals now extinct; and it continues with Spaniards, Frenchmen, and Americans exploring this wilderness during the early historic period. You will sense the daring of swift-riding Kiowa and Comanche lancers charging into a herd of buffalo on the Oklahoma prairies. Perhaps you will share the suffering of the Five Civilized Tribes on their "Trail of Tears" to Oklahoma, or feel the danger of scouting with Cherokee General Stand Watie's raiders during the Civil War, driving a herd of Texas longhorn cattle up the Chisholm Trail to the Kansas cow towns, or racing for a homestead in the Cherokee Outlet. You may endure with the Sooners the hardships of opening pioneer farms and building new towns on the Oklahoma frontier. And, finally, you will appreciate the miracle of the transformation of Oklahoma from a wilderness territory to a modern American state.

Several Reader Aids are included to help you get the most out of this book. Study the illustrations as carefully as you do the printed pages. Each is related to some important part of the story you are reading. Also refer to the maps each time a river, mountain, meridian, or boundary is mentioned. Knowing where these points are located will improve your understanding of Oklahoma history.

Two Reader Aids are placed at the end of the book—"Proper Names and Terms" and "Definitions." The story of Oklahoma is more complex than that of most of the other states. It requires the use of names of persons, places, and terms which often are difficult to pronounce. These are listed in the "Proper Names and Terms" section. Each proper name, place, or term is divided and accented. This story also requires words that may be new to you.

These words are listed in the "Definitions" section. With each word listed is its meaning or definition.

Use these Reader Aids—the illustrations, maps, Proper Names and Terms, and Definitions. You'll get more out of *The Oklahoma Story*. You will more fully appreciate the drama, excitement, and achievement of the Oklahoma heritage.

ARRELL MORGAN GIBSON

Norman, Oklahoma

Contents

Illustrations

MAPS

All the maps in this book are from *Historical Atlas of Oklahoma,* Second Edition, by John W. Morris, Charles R. Goins, and Edwin C. McReynolds, published by the University of Oklahoma Press.

The
Oklahoma
Story

CHAPTER ONE

The People of Oklahoma

Oklahoma today is the home of nearly three million people. They are red people, black people, and white people.

Red people, the Indians, were Oklahoma's first settlers. Their ancestors entered Oklahoma 15,000 to 20,000 years ago. They hunted and farmed until they were forced to share Oklahoma with settlers from the eastern United States. Today, Indians in Oklahoma are doctors, lawyers, teachers, and leaders in state politics. Indians excel in painting, writing, and ballet and tribal dancing. Also, many Indians are skilled craftsmen.

Blacks arrived in Oklahoma around 1830. They were brought as slaves by the Chero-kees, Creeks, Choctaws, Seminoles, and Chick-asaws. Black slaves tended crops, built roads, and labored to open the Oklahoma wilderness. At the close of the Civil War in 1865, all slaves were freed, and Oklahoma blacks began the slow and difficult movement to gain equality. For many years after gaining freedom they were suppressed in Oklahoma and in other parts of the South and Southwest. However, since the Supreme Court's ruling against segregation in 1954, blacks have begun to share equally in Oklahoma education and to have a larger part in economic and political life. Oklahoma blacks have contributed to literature, including poetry, and to entertainment. Blacks

1. Glass Mountains, in Major County, Oklahoma.

2. Wichita Mountains.

now serve in state and local government, and many blacks are teachers, lawyers, and doctors.

Whites first came to Oklahoma as explorers. Spaniards visited Oklahoma in 1541. French and American explorers came after the Spaniards. A few white traders, trappers, and soldiers also came to Oklahoma before 1830. In 1889 Oklahoma was opened to homesteaders. Then many whites, most of them farmers, settled in Oklahoma.

After 1889, whites dominated Oklahoma business, professional, political, and social life. However, whites today share the stage with Indians and blacks. Indian, black, and white men and women all now serve Oklahoma as lawmakers, judges, writers, doctors, educators, scientists, farmers, ranchers, factory workers, craftsmen, and social leaders.

THE FIRST OKLAHOMANS

People have lived here for 20,000 years, yet Oklahoma had no written records until 1541, when explorers from Spain arrived. That period in Oklahoma's past from about 20,000 years ago down to 1541 is called the Prehistoric Age. Scientists who study the Prehistoric Age are called archaeologists. Archaeologists piece together the unwritten record of Oklahoma's Prehistoric Age by studying weapons, tools, pottery, and stone carvings made by early Oklahomans. They use the carbon-14 test (which measures the radioactive life of ancient materials) and dendrochronology (the study of tree rings in wood found in ancient villages) to determine the age of prehistoric remains. Archaeologists have found that Oklahoma was widely inhabited by people during the Prehistoric Age.

The Strange Environment—The story of Oklahomans changing their environment from a wilderness to a modern American state is an exciting drama. It begins nearly 20,000 years ago at the time Oklahoma's first settlers, the Indians' ancestors, migrated to this area. Then Oklahoma's natural environment was different from the way it is today. When the first settlers entered Oklahoma they found it was mostly flat. Here and there low mountains rose above the prairies. They were the Glass Mountains in northwestern Oklahoma, the Wichita Mountains in southwestern Oklahoma, and the Arbuckle Mountains in south-central Oklahoma. But eastern Oklahoma was much rougher.

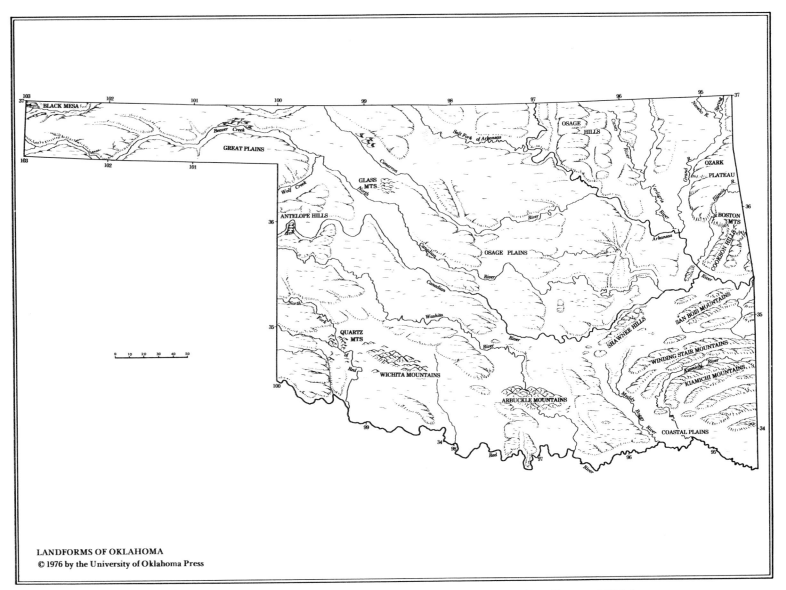

Landforms of Oklahoma

3. Skeleton of Columbian Mammoth exhibited in the Stovall Museum.

Much of the land was rugged hills. The Ozark Mountains were in northeastern Oklahoma. The Ouachita (Kiamichi) Mountains were in southeastern Oklahoma. Oklahoma's present river system had been formed. The Arkansas River and its tributaries—the Salt Fork, Cimarron, Canadian, Verdigris, Grand, and Illinois rivers—drained northern Oklahoma. The Red River and its tributaries—the North Fork, Washita, Blue, and Kiamichi rivers—drained southern Oklahoma.

The greatest difference in the Oklahoma environment 20,000 years ago was in its climate, plants, and wild life. During most of the Prehistoric Age, the climate was influenced by a huge glacier. It was a vast sheet of ice which extended from the North Pole into the northern edge of the United States. The ice sheet made Oklahoma's climate mild. Heavy rain fell every year. Thick, tall grass and large trees grew all across Oklahoma. Several types of wild animals lived in Oklahoma during the Ice Age. The Columbian mammoth, a huge creature which resembled an elephant, and small horses and camels were numerous. These animals are now extinct.

Early Oklahomans—Oklahoma's earliest people were hunters. They roamed the land searching for the Columbian mammoth and other prehistoric creatures for food and hides to use for clothing. Archaeologists have found three types of early man in Oklahoma. These pioneer Oklahomans, ancestors of the Indian, are called Plainview man, Clovis man, and Folsom man. They lived in caves and shelters and under rock ledges. Many of these early shelters can be seen in the high bluffs along Oklahoma's creeks and rivers. The people hunted near swamps and water holes for mammoths and other animals. Earliest of Oklahoma's big game hunters was Clovis man. He hunted across Oklahoma over 15,000 years ago. Plainview man was next and lived in Oklahoma as late as 10,000 years ago. Folsom man was the most recent Oklahoma resident during the glacial period of the Prehistoric Age. He was present here as late as 8,000 years ago.

Clovis man, Plainview man, and Folsom man were skilled in making stone points for lances and spears. They used these weapons to kill game animals and to protect themselves from invading hunters. Oklahoma's Prehistoric Age settlers made points for their lances and spears

9

and scrapers. Flint deposits are found in northeastern Oklahoma in present Ottawa County.

THE PALEO PEOPLE

With the gradual melting of the huge glacier, the Ice Age came to an end about 8,000 years ago. At the same time, Oklahoma's climate began to change. As the climate changed, plants and animals changed, too. Ice Age trees, shrubs, and grasses, and such animals as the Columbian mammoth, horse, and camel disappeared. Gradually plants—trees, shrubs, and grasses—and animals—deer, antelope, bison or buffalo, and other creatures—found here today became common.

People continued to live in Oklahoma during this period of environmental change. Archaeologists call them Paleo People. This period in Oklahoma, still in the Prehistoric Age, could also be called the Stone Age. Weapons and tools used by the Paleo People were made of stone.

Changing Culture—The Paleo People adapted to the new environment. For several thousand years they continued to live as wandering hunters. But changes began to take place in their way of living or their life style. Life

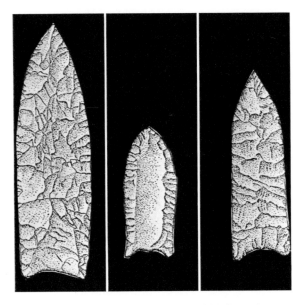

4. Weapon points produced by Oklahoma's earliest known settlers. *Left to right:* Clovis, Folsom, and Plainview.

from a hard stone called flint. Early hunters placed chunks of flint in camp fires. Heat caused the flint to flake into thin sheets. Then, by chipping, prehistoric craftsmen shaped the flint flakes into spear points, crude knives, style is culture. Archaeologists divide culture in two parts. One is material culture. It is things made by man. These things include tools, weapons, pottery, baskets and other containers for storing and cooking food, clothing, and shelter. The other part of culture is non-material. Religion, family, and government are examples of non-material culture.

Paleo Oklahomans improved their material culture by improving their food supply. Later their material culture was strong enough to improve their non-material culture in art, religion, and government.

Paleo Life Style—Paleo Oklahomans hunted deer, antelope, buffalo, and other wild animals. They also began to gather seeds, berries, and nuts from shrubs and trees. They had more food than their Clovis, Plainview, and Folsom ancestors. Paleo Oklahomans learned to preserve and store food to be used during periods when food was scarce. Their skills in making weapons, tools, and household goods improved. This helped them to become even better hunters and food gatherers.

The Paleo Indian population increased. Scattered families began to collect in groups called bands. Soon they formed larger groups

5. Prehistoric drawings on the bluffs of Cimarron Canyon, Oklahoma Panhandle.

called tribes. Paleo Oklahomans found that it was safer to live in larger groups. They could protect themselves better from attack by fierce animals and enemy invaders. Then Paleo Oklahomans moved out of the caves and ledges during the spring and summer and spent more time traveling about the country collecting food. These early-day Oklahomans camped near creeks or on riverbanks, generally near salt springs. During winter they returned to

11

6. Prehistoric cliff markings near Black Mesa, Oklahoma Panhandle.

sites. Over several thousand years this camp material collected and formed into layers. Wind and flood water carried soil which covered the cave and ledge floors and the riverbank campsites. In several Oklahoma caves in the Ozarks and in the Panhandle near Kenton, this camp material with its dirt cover was nearly ten feet deep. Similar deposits built up along many streams in the state.

Digging through these early homesites, archaeologists excavate stone spear points, knives, scrapers, grinders, bone fishhooks, seeds and nuts, charcoal, and pieces of wood. From these they piece together the story of Paleo Oklahomans. They use the carbon-14 test and dendrochronology to date the material. This is the only way we can get information on the Prehistoric Age of Oklahoma. Since the Paleo People did not have a system of writing, they had no way to leave a written record. Therefore, knowledge of their life style must be drawn from archaeological evidence.

Age of the Moundbuilders—During the late Prehistoric Age, about 500 B.C. to A.D. 900, important changes took place among the peo-

their cave and ledge homes for protection against cold winds and snow.

Paleo Indians left camp material in the cave and ledge homes and at the riverbank camp-

12

7. Artist's drawing of an Ozark ledge dwellers site, showing habitation layers.

In river valleys, workmen built mounds as platforms on which they placed houses. This kept homes from being washed away by floods. Oklahoma builders built their houses of frames made from trunks of small trees lashed together with pieces of strong bark. They covered the sides with plaster made from clay and water, made stronger with small sticks. These early Oklahomans roofed their homes with woven fiber mats.

Many of the mounds, nearly fifty feet high, were built as religious pyramids. Some of them were solid and probably were used as temples. Other mounds were built over strong cedar frames. These were used as burial vaults.

The Spiro Age—The Golden Age of Oklahoma Prehistory took place during the period 900 to 1450. The Oklahomans of this age are called the Spiro People. They excelled all other Moundbuilders. Spiro People had superior skill in building, in engineering, in farming, and in government. Their farms produced rich crops of corn, beans, squash, and melons. Spiro craftsmen made fine cloth and pottery and worked with copper, shell, and stone.

Little was known about the Spiro People

ple of Oklahoma. Archaeologists call this period the Moundbuilders Age. Early Oklahomans built mounds throughout the state.

13

8. Spiro Mounds site before excavation.

14

9. Etched tortoise-shell neck ornaments called gorgets, Spiro Mounds artifacts.

until recently. During the 1930's in the Arkansas River valley of eastern Oklahoma, prospectors dug into a hill searching for coal. The hill proved to be an ancient burial mound containing valuable shell, stone, ceramic, and textile artifacts. The miners plundered many of Spiro Mound's treasures and sold them to collectors and dealers. In searching through the burial chambers and blasting tunnels with dynamite to open new chambers, they damaged the mound and destroyed many artifacts. Before the miners completely emptied Spiro

15

10. Two sculptured stone pipes, Spiro Mounds artifacts.

Mound of its riches, the Oklahoma legislature passed a law which made this ancient Indian shrine state property. Then professional archaeologists were permitted to study Spiro Mound. Their careful examination of the burial chambers and their contents disclosed that Spiro builders had created the huge mound by forming the inside of strong cedar logs. Paleo Indian workmen had covered the log frame with thousands of tons of dirt carried to the mound in containers of animal skins and woven fibers. When completed, Spiro Mound was a large hill nearly fifty feet high.

The Spiro People left no written record. Yet it is possible to tell something about their life style. The mound itself tells several important things. Spiro Mound, like the pyramids of Egypt, is an example of engineering knowledge and construction ability. The artifacts taken from Spiro Mound also tell much about these people. The life story of the Spiro People, worked out by archaeologists studying the evidence taken from Spiro Mound, tells of early-day Oklahomans relating to their environment. It also tells of contacts with other Paleo Indian peoples through trade. Objects from Spiro Mound tell of an advanced

11. Carved stone caricature, Spiro Mounds artifact.

17

life style for Oklahomans during the period 900 to 1450. The Spiro People lived in large communities supported by a prosperous agriculture. Their principal crops were corn, beans, melons, pumpkins, squash, and tobacco.

The towns of the Spiro nation were held together by a central government. Spiro craftsmen had special skills. They made fine pottery and cloth and carved stone figures and worked in metal. Spiro merchants traded with other Paleo Indian nations. Conch shells and pearls came from the Gulf of Mexico, and copper was received from the Great Lakes area. Objects made from these materials were placed in Spiro Mound. Scholars call this period in Indian history the Stone Age, although the Spiro People used copper to make tools, weapons, and pieces for their households and for personal adornment.

Objects taken from the Spiro Mound burial chamber include decorated pottery, cedar masks, human and animal figures carved from stone, clay and stone pipes, and pearl and

12. Ceramic decanter, Spiro Mounds artifact.

shell beads. Household items include baskets and other woven utensils, pieces of cooking and storage pottery, textiles with colorful designs, and blankets of buffalo hair, rabbit fur, and feathers. Archaeologists also found cane combs, polished stone implements and weapons, decorated conch shells, and copper shields, axes, and ear ornaments in the mound.

The Spiro nation and its high culture had vanished by 1541, when European explorers entered Oklahoma. Many scholars believe that about 1450 the Spiro nation was destroyed by Paleo Indian raiders from the Western Plains.

Oklahoma's Historic Indian Setting—By the time that Europeans discovered Oklahoma in 1541, it was already the home of several Indian tribes. On the Red and Arkansas rivers lived the Caddoan People, ancestors of the present-day Wichitas and Caddoes. They lived in farming villages. Corn was their most important crop. The Caddoan People constructed dome-shaped houses made of bent poles formed into a semi-circle, lashed with strong bark, and covered with large, water-tight mats woven from cattails.

The Quapaw tribe lived on the lower Ar-

13. Excavation work on the Spiro Mounds.

kansas and Red rivers. They farmed and hunted. When the Europeans arrived in Oklahoma, the Quapaws resided near the territory of the Spiro People.

19

14. Running buffalo herd.

20

15.   Buffalo herd in the Wichita Mountains Wildlife Refuge.

On the prairies of western Oklahoma lived the Plains Apaches. They had no permanent villages like the Caddoans and Quapaws. The Plains Apaches were migratory, moving from place to place, following the buffalo herds. Plains Apaches had no agriculture, but depended entirely upon the buffalo.

The coming of the Europeans marked the end of the Prehistoric Age in Oklahoma. European explorers brought a system of writing. They wrote about Oklahoma and the native peoples. These first written records for this region mark the opening of Oklahoma's Historic Age.

21

CHAPTER TWO

Europeans in Oklahoma

About 1500 the economic life of many European nations was changing. Europeans were shifting from agriculture to industry and commerce. This change caused European cities to increase in population. People moved from the country, where they had been farmers, to the cities, where they became daily wage earners.

Europe's new industries required raw materials. Leaders of the European nations wished to find new sources of raw materials—minerals, wood products, animal skins and furs, and food—for the industrial cities. They also wished to reduce the surplus population in some of the more crowded cities.

These needs led Europeans to seek lands across the sea. Colonies would supply raw materials. Also, colonies would provide places to settle surplus population. About the year 1500, after inventors had improved sailing ships, Europeans were eager to explore the world. Between 1500 and 1600, daring sailors explored most of the islands and the mainland of the New World. After discovery of the new territory, explorers searched for places to establish colonies. Several of these explorations led Europeans to Oklahoma.

SPANIARDS IN OKLAHOMA

In the early years of European discovery the Spaniards were the most successful. They were the pioneer explorers of the present United States. Christopher Columbus discovered the Caribbean Islands in 1492. Spaniards established settlements in these islands. They used the islands as bases for expanding their empire in the New World. In 1519, Spanish soldiers began the conquest of Mexico, finally defeating the Aztec Indians. After they were established in Mexico, the Spaniards began to explore the territory north of Mexico City. Their explorations led to the discovery of Oklahoma.

The Coronado Expedition—Spaniards asked the Mexican Indians to describe the territory north of Mexico City. The natives told the Europeans that far to the north were three kingdoms. Each kingdom was rich in gold, silver, and pearls. The Mexican Indians told the Spaniards that these kingdoms were called Cíbola, Quivira, and Cale.

According to the Indian stories, Cíbola was the richest of the three centers of wealth. Cíbola's outer wall was constructed of solid gold. Doors of the shops and houses were covered with turquoise. The people of Cíbola, according to the Mexican Indian stories, lived in luxury. In Cale the men wore hats of gold and pearl jewelry. Quivira was farther north

16. Artist's sketch of men from Coronado's expedition.

23

than Cíbola and Cale. It was a land where gold and silver were plentiful. The natives made weapons from silver. Women served their men from golden pitchers. Tiny golden bells tinkled on the branches of shade trees. Children wore gold bracelets on their arms and legs.

The Spaniards believed these Indian fables and were eager to visit Cíbola, Cale, and Quivira. They formed several expeditions to search for these northern kingdoms. Francisco Vasquez de Coronado was the leader of one expedition. In February, 1540, he set out from Compostela, on the west coast of Mexico, with nearly 1,500 Spaniards and Indians in his exploring party. After many weeks of wandering across mountains and deserts, Coronado and his men finally reached Cíbola in western New Mexico. Cíbola was a large settlement of Indians. They lived in tall adobe and stone buildings. But Cíbola was a disappointment to Coronado. He found no gold or silver there.

Coronado rested his men at Cíbola, then he began the search for Quivira. The Spaniards explored eastern New Mexico and the Texas Panhandle. During 1541 they entered western Oklahoma, where they hunted buffalo and visited the camps of the Plains Apaches. These Plains Apaches were the first Indians that the Spaniards met in Oklahoma.

Coronado explored western Oklahoma, then marched his men to the Arkansas River in south-central Kansas. There the Spaniards found the kingdom of Quivira, but again they were disappointed. Quivira was not a center of great wealth. The Europeans found no gold or silver there. Quivirans were Wichita Indians. They lived in settlements of dome-shaped houses covered with woven grass mats. The Quivirans were skillful farmers. They raised corn, beans, squash, and pumpkins.

The Spaniards rested at Quivira and prepared to return to Mexico. Before he ordered the homeward march, Coronado gave permission to a small group of missionaries to remain. The missionaries wished to work among the Indians. They lived here for several years trying to teach the Indian tribes of Oklahoma about Christianity.

The Spaniards found no gold or silver in Cíbola and Quivira. Yet their expedition was important in the history of this region. Coronado and his men were the first Europeans to

17. Artist's sketch of Spaniard from the Coronado expedition and his Indian guide, searching for Quivira.

visit Oklahoma. Their reports of the land and people are the first written records of Oklahoma. They ended Oklahoma's Prehistoric Age and began the Historic Age. Coronado claimed this territory as a part of the Spanish empire. The flag of Spain had come to Oklahoma.

The De Soto Expedition—While Coronado and his men wandered across the Southwest, Spaniards were exploring other parts of the present United States. One expedition was led by Hernando de Soto. De Soto's men explored the lower Mississippi Valley in search of the kingdom of Cale.

De Soto came no farther west than present Little Rock, Arkansas. He had some contact with the Chickasaws, Choctaws, Creeks, and other tribes then living in the southeastern United States. Later these tribes were settled in Oklahoma. The De Soto expedition introduced these tribes to horses, firearms, tools, and European ways.

Spanish Interest in Oklahoma—Spanish interest in the territory north of Mexico continued. In 1598 Spanish settlers from Mexico moved

25

into New Mexico and established several towns near the Río Grande, the "Great River." One of these settlements, founded in 1609, was Santa Fe, which became the capital of Spanish territory in the Southwest. Juan de Oñate was the leader of these Spanish colonists.

Spaniards still believed the Indian fables of rich kingdoms on the northern frontier. From their settlements in New Mexico, they continued to search for Cíbola, Quivira, and Cale. Several of these expeditions crossed Oklahoma. One from New Mexico in 1601, was led by Oñate, who explored into central Oklahoma along the valley of the Canadian River in search of Quivira.

The Spaniards established stock raising in New Mexico. Soon Spanish ranches had herds of sheep, cattle, and horses. Many horses escaped from the New Mexico ranches. These animals formed into wild herds and roamed the plains into western Oklahoma. Oklahoma Indians captured horses from these herds and learned to use them for carrying riders and household goods. With horses, Oklahoma Indians could move more easily over a wider territory. They became better hunters in taking the buffalo.

About 1700, two Indian tribes from the north, the Comanches and Kiowas, migrated to Oklahoma. They settled in the Wichita Mountains. The Comanches and Kiowas adopted the horse. They hunted buffalo and raided Spanish settlements in Texas, northern Mexico, and New Mexico.

Spaniards from New Mexico often came to Oklahoma to trade with the Comanches and Kiowas. Sometimes Spanish armies invaded western Oklahoma to punish the Comanches and Kiowas for raiding their towns in New Mexico.

The Spaniards did not establish settlements in Oklahoma. Yet they claimed Oklahoma as a part of their territory in North America, and they visited Oklahoma to explore and to hunt buffalo.

FRENCHMEN IN OKLAHOMA

Soon after Spain established colonies in North America, France began to show interest in the New World. Eventually the French flag came to Oklahoma. Spaniards had entered Oklahoma from Mexico and from their towns in New Mexico. Frenchmen reached Oklahoma from the north and east.

Frenchmen first established colonies in Canada along the St. Lawrence River. French explorers and traders moved across the Great Lakes. By the 1650's, Frenchmen had reached the Mississippi River and soon were exploring the territory along the Mississippi River to the Gulf of Mexico. These explorations led them into Oklahoma.

French Explorations in the Southwest—The first French exploration along the Mississippi River occurred in 1673. With five Indian guides, Louis Joliet, a trader, and Father Marquette, a missionary, set out from Lake Michigan in two canoes. They followed a route that took them to the Wisconsin River. By that stream they entered the upper Mississippi River. Drifting down the Mississippi River, Joliet and Marquette explored to the mouth of the Arkansas River before returning to Canada.

The second, and the most important, French exploration of the Mississippi Valley occurred in 1682. Robert Cavelier, Sieur de la Salle led an expedition down the Mississippi River to the Gulf of Mexico. The territory on the west bank of the Mississippi River he named Louisi-

18. Indian encampment with skin lodges. War shield on tripod in foreground.

ana in honor of his king, Louis XIV. La Salle planned to tap the rich fur resources of Louisiana. He believed that Louisiana would become the most important colony in the French

27

empire in North America. La Salle attempted to carry out his plan to settle and develop Louisiana.

The La Salle plan for Louisiana succeeded in 1699. In that year, two brothers named Iberville and Bienville Le Moyne led an expedition to the mouth of the Mississippi River. They founded the city of Biloxi near the Gulf of Mexico. In 1718, Bienville le Moyne founded New Orleans, situated about 100 miles from the mouth of the Mississippi River.

French Settlements in Oklahoma—From New Orleans, large numbers of French traders moved up the Red, Arkansas, Canadian, Grand, and Verdigris rivers. They planned to establish the fur trade in Oklahoma and other parts of Louisiana. The first Frenchman to visit Oklahoma was Juchereau de St. Denis. In 1714 he explored the land drained by Red River. St. Denis was searching for spots to establish settlements in order to trade with the Indian tribes.

During 1719, Bernard de la Harpe led another expedition from New Orleans to the Indian towns on the Canadian River in eastern Oklahoma. These were settlements of Wichitas and Caddoes. They had formerly lived on the Arkansas River in south-central Kansas. Their Kansas settlements were called Quivira. Soon after Coronado visited them in 1541, they had moved to eastern Oklahoma. Some of the Wichitas and Caddoes had settled to the south on Red River. Spaniards called these Indians Quivirans. Frenchmen called them Taovayas.

La Harpe kept a journal record of his visit to eastern Oklahoma. He described the prosperity of the Wichitas and Caddoes. La Harpe was impressed by their fields of corn, pumpkins, beans, and tobacco scattered on the fertile river bottoms around their villages. He wrote that the Taovayas cultivated great quantities of tobacco. They pressed the dried tobacco into flat loaves and used it for trade with other Indian tribes.

La Harpe found that the Taovayas raised fine horses. They made saddles, bridles, and armor from tough buffalo-hide leather. La Harpe learned that each October the Taovayas left their villages to hunt buffalo on the plains of western Oklahoma. They returned in March to plant their crops.

La Harpe was impressed with Oklahoma.

28

19. French fur traders shoot the rapids.

He wrote in his journal that it was the best trade area in the French colony of Louisiana. He noted that Oklahoma's forests and prairies abounded in fur-bearing animals. La Harpe recommended that French traders tap Oklahoma's rich fur resources. He said that Oklahoma's climate was mild, its land was fertile, and there were rich minerals and abundant furs. It surpassed all other regions of the colony of Louisiana. During La Harpe's visit, Frenchmen and Indians raised the French flag over the Taovaya villages.

French traders soon appeared in Oklahoma. They erected trading posts among the Taovayas. Frenchmen easily adapted to life in the Oklahoma wilderness. They lived in the Indian villages and married Indian women. They also established trading settlements. The largest French town in Oklahoma was Ferdinandina on the Arkansas River near present Newkirk. San Bernardo and San Teodoro, called Twin Villages, situated on Red River in present Jefferson County, also were large settlements.

Each year French traders made large canoes from huge, hollowed-out, cottonwood logs. They called these boats pirogues. The French traders traveled in their pirogues on the Arkansas and Red and Mississippi rivers to New Orleans. There they loaded cargoes of guns, ammunition, knives, beads, axes, hatchets, hoes, cloth, and blankets and returned to Oklahoma. The traders exchanged these goods with Indian hunters for pelts and hides. Each year the traders transported out of Oklahoma many bales of beaver, otter, mink, and muskrat furs and tanned buffalo robes. At New Orleans the bales of furs and hides were loaded on large ships waiting to depart for Europe. These furs and hides were in great demand in France. There workmen made them into hats, coats, shoes, and boots.

The French prospered in Oklahoma. Traders carried on a rich commerce with the Taovayas. Later Frenchmen wished to trade with the Comanches and Kiowas who roamed western Oklahoma. These Indians had buffalo robes and hides to trade. They also raided Spanish settlements in northern Mexico, Texas, and New Mexico. Their plunder included horses, mules, and gold and silver. Most Frenchmen were afraid to go onto the plains to trade with these fierce Indians. They hired Taovaya Indians to visit the Comanche and

Kiowa villages. They exchanged guns, knives, and blankets for buffalo robes and hides, horses, mules, and plunder.

SHIFTING CONTROL OF OKLAHOMA

By 1750 French and Taovaya traders were very influential with the Comanches and Kiowas, supplying them with guns and ammunition. The Comanches and Kiowas used these weapons to raid Spanish settlements. Spanish officials planned to end this threat to their northern frontier. They established settlements in Texas, and they placed more soldiers in northern Mexico and in New Mexico.

Several times, Spanish armies from Texas and New Mexico invaded Oklahoma. They wished to punish the Comanches and Kiowas and to expel the French. The largest Spanish effort took place in 1759. Diego Parilla was the commander of the Spanish fort at San Saba, in Texas. He marched an army of 300 soldiers north to Red River. In early October, 1759, Parilla's army reached Twin Villages. The Spaniards attacked the settlement with great fury. French and Taovaya defenders bravely fought back. After a bloody battle that lasted all day, Frenchmen and Taovayas defeated the Spaniards and forced them to retreat. The battle of Twin Villages was the largest conflict to take place in Oklahoma during the eighteenth century.

Return of Oklahoma to Spain—In 1762 French and Spanish leaders signed a treaty. It required France to return Louisiana to Spain. Thus in 1762 the Spanish flag returned to Oklahoma.

Spanish control over Oklahoma, as a part of the colony of Louisiana, was slight. Spanish officials governed this territory from New Orleans and from San Antonio. They tried to check the French traders who remained in Oklahoma. The Spanish government wished to stop French traders from supplying guns and ammunition to the Comanches and Kiowas. The Spaniards constructed roads across Oklahoma to connect towns in Texas with settlements in New Mexico. One road linking San Antonio and Santa Fe crossed western Oklahoma.

Return of Louisiana to France—In 1800 a treaty between the French and Spanish governments required the return of Louisiana, including Oklahoma, to France. But France

31

took only slight interest in the colony, and for three years Louisiana had little control from the French government.

In 1803, ownership of Louisiana and Oklahoma changed again. The young United States owned the territory from the Atlantic Ocean to the east bank of the Mississippi River. American officials in 1803 signed a treaty with French officials. The treaty provided for the purchase of Louisiana by the United States for $15,000,000. With this purchase the American flag came to Oklahoma in 1803.

CHAPTER THREE

American Pioneers in Oklahoma

In 1803, Oklahoma became United States territory. For some time Americans referred to most of the land west of the Mississippi River as Louisiana. That had been its name when it was a French colony and, later, a Spanish colony. Gradually the United States government began to divide Louisiana into states. In 1812, Congress created the state of Louisiana. The remainder of the American territory west of the Mississippi River was called Missouri Territory. Through the years, other portions of the old colony of Louisiana were divided into states, one of which was Arkansas. Congress created Indian Territory about 1825, and that remained the name for Oklahoma until 1889, when a portion of Indian Territory became Oklahoma Territory.

OKLAHOMA ON THE EVE OF AMERICAN SETTLEMENT

Soon after 1803, explorers, soldiers, and private citizens entered Oklahoma. Explorers came to study the land and resources, and to map Oklahoma. Soldiers came to build forts and to guard the Oklahoma frontier. Spain still owned Texas and New Mexico. Two types of private citizens came to Oklahoma after 1803. Settlers came to establish farms and towns. Trappers and traders came to hunt fur-bearing animals and to supply Indians with goods.

The Wilderness Setting—These American pioneers found Oklahoma very attractive. The long period of French and Spanish rule had not depleted Oklahoma's vast natural resources. European and Indian hunters had not exhausted the supply of wild animals. Great numbers of beaver, otter, mink, and bear remained. Deer and elk roamed the Oklahoma prairies, and huge herds of buffalo grazed on the plains of western Oklahoma. Turkeys, quail, rabbits, squirrels, and other game birds and animals were plentiful.

Oklahoma's forests of pine, cedar, oak, hickory, gum, and walnut trees had hardly been touched by the Europeans. Scattered about Oklahoma were easily-mined minerals required by pioneers. These minerals were lead, coal, and salt. Lead was used for making bullets. Frontier blacksmiths used coal to fire their forges in order to shoe horses, mules, and oxen. They also repaired metal parts of wagons and other pioneer equipment. Pioneers required salt to flavor food and to preserve meat.

Oklahoma's many creeks and rivers provided pioneers a dependable supply of fresh water for drinking, cooking, and washing clothes. Water power turned the mills to grind grain into meal and flour and to saw lumber. These streams had many fish, which pioneers could catch and use for food.

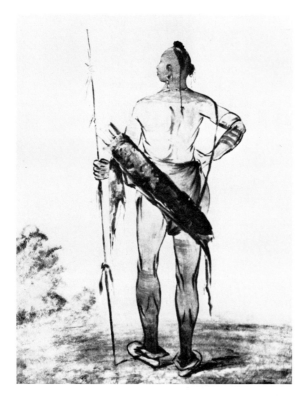

20. Pawhuska, an Osage warrior, painted by George Catlin.

34

21. Comanche village scene.

The Indian Setting—Pioneers entering Oklahoma after 1803 found several Indian tribes living here. Osages were powerful people who roamed northeastern Oklahoma. Their warriors were large and strong, had great courage and terrible fury in battle, and were feared by Indians of other tribes. The Osages numbered nearly 5,000. They were at war with all the tribes in the Southwest.

Quapaws resided in eastern Oklahoma in the territory between the Arkansas and Red rivers. They spoke a language similar to the Osages', but they were more peaceful than the Osages. For many years the Quapaws had been in close contact with Frenchmen and Spaniards. Many times they had suffered epidemics of measles, smallpox, and other European diseases. In 1803, when the United States acquired Louisiana, the Quapaw population was less than 1,000.

West of the Osages and Quapaws lived the Wichitas and Caddoes. From historic times they had resided in southern Kansas and Oklahoma, called Quivirans by the Spaniards and called Taovayas by the French. During 1719, Bernard de la Harpe visited their villages near the mouth of the Canadian River in eastern Oklahoma, but Osage raids forced the Wichitas and Caddoes to move south to Red River. Their settlements were near the French trading post of Twin Villages. When the Americans acquired Oklahoma, many Wichitas and Caddoes were moving to the Wichita Mountains.

Also living in western Oklahoma were the Plains Apaches. Indians from this tribe were the first to meet the Spaniards when they explored Oklahoma during 1541. At the time of the American takeover of Louisiana, the Plains Apaches numbered about 300.

Near the year 1700, two fierce tribes from the north, the Comanches and Kiowas, migrated to western Oklahoma. Most of the time their villages were situated in the Wichita Mountains.

After Oklahoma became American territory, all of these Indian people influenced the history of the region. The Osages, Comanches, and Kiowas fiercely resisted the American pioneers.

AMERICAN EXPLORERS IN OKLAHOMA

The vast western territory which the United States acquired in 1803 had no definite west-

22. Kiowa hunting camp, showing buffalo meat drying on frames.

ern boundary. There was uncertainty as to where United States territory ended and Spanish territory began. The lack of a definite border created difficulty between the United States and Spain, and American leaders were anxious to have this matter settled. They believed that either the Arkansas River or the Red River would become the boundary separating Spanish and American territory.

President Thomas Jefferson was eager to have Louisiana explored and mapped. Jefferson directed the secretary of war to use the army to explore Louisiana. Other presidents continued this practice until the boundary question was finally settled in 1821. Many of the explorations crossed Oklahoma.

The Sparks Expedition—During 1806 the secretary of war ordered Captain Richard Sparks to explore the Red River to its source. Sparks planned to move his men in three small boats to Twin Villages on the upper Red River. There he hoped the Wichita and Caddo Indians would supply him with horses for continuing the westward journey.

On June 2, 1806, Sparks and a party of twenty-four men left Natchitoches in present

23. Thomas Jefferson in 1800, as painted by Rembrandt Peale.

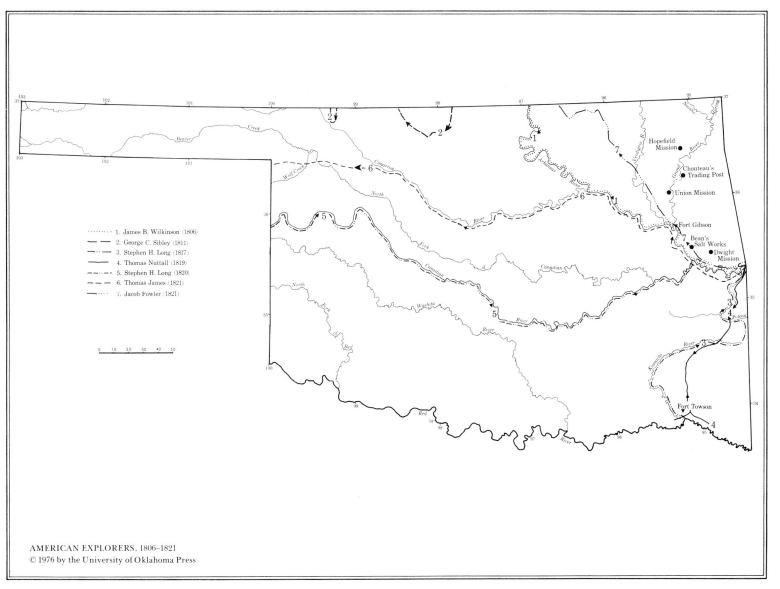

American Explorers in Oklahoma, 1806–1821

Legend:

1. James B. Wilkinson (1806)
2. George C. Sibley (1811)
3. Stephen H. Long (1817)
4. Thomas Nuttall (1819)
5. Stephen H. Long (1820)
6. Thomas James (1821)
7. Jacob Fowler (1821)

Louisiana and moved slowly upstream. Just as the Americans reached the southeastern corner of Oklahoma, they were met by a large force of Spanish soldiers. These troops were from the Spanish fort at Nacogdoches, situated in east Texas. The Spaniards claimed that the Americans were trespassing on Spanish territory and ordered Sparks and his men to turn back.

The Sparks expedition was a failure, because Americans were unable to reach the headwaters of Red River. But it was important in Oklahoma history, because Sparks was the first American official to reach Oklahoma.

The Pike Expedition—In 1806 also, the secretary of war ordered an army expedition to explore the Arkansas River. Captain Zebulon M. Pike was placed in command of twenty-three men. Lieutenant James Wilkinson was a member of the party. The explorers left St. Louis during the summer of 1806. They traveled by boat up the Missouri River and the Osage River to southwest Missouri. Pike then marched his men to the Osage villages. There he purchased horses to continue the journey across the plains.

24.   Zebulon M. Pike.

The Americans explored Kansas to the great bend of the Arkansas River. There Pike ordered Lieutenant Wilkinson to take five men and descend the Arkansas River to its mouth on the Mississippi River. Wilkinson and his men constructed two boats.

On October 28, 1806, the expedition divided. Captain Pike rode west with his column toward the Rocky Mountains. Lieutenant Wilkinson and his men launched their boats into the Arkansas River. They drifted with the current in a southeasterly direction and spent November and December in Oklahoma.

Winter came early in 1806. The weather was severe, and Wilkinson's boats capsized several times. Men and supplies were thrown into the cold water. Ice on the river slowed their passage. In places, ice extended from bank to bank, and Wilkinson's men had to break the ice with axes so the boats could pass. Sometimes ice drifted in huge, crunching chunks. Wilkinson and his men suffered many hardships. Finally, on New Year's Day, 1807, they reached Belle Point on the eastern border of Oklahoma. Then they moved more easily along the Arkansas River to the Mississippi River.

Lieutenant Wilkinson kept a journal in which he described his explorations along the Arkansas River. It was the first American account of northeastern Oklahoma. Wilkinson reported passing several Osage villages and hunting camps and meeting American trappers and traders.

The Sibley Expedition—The Sparks and Wilkinson explorations in Oklahoma were followed by the Sibley expedition. George C. Sibley was Indian agent at Fort Osage, Missouri. During May, 1811, with several Osage guides he explored portions of northern Oklahoma. Sibley entered Oklahoma along the valley of the Arkansas River and explored the land on the tributaries of the Arkansas River in northern Oklahoma. He observed the Salt Fork, Cimarron, and Chikaskia rivers. Sibley was impressed by Oklahoma's Great Salt Plains. He reported that they glistened "like a brilliant field of snow in the summer sun" on the banks of the Salt Fork River.

The Long Expedition—Major Stephen H. Long explored Oklahoma twice. In 1817 the secretary of war ordered Major Long to select a site on the Arkansas River for a fort. He chose

25. George C. Sibley.

Belle Point, located on the high bluffs at the junction of the Poteau River and the Arkansas River. The post constructed at Belle Point became Fort Smith. While in Oklahoma in 1817, Long explored from Fort Smith across southeastern Oklahoma by way of the Kiamichi Mountains to Red River.

In 1819 the secretary of war sent Major Long on another assignment. He was to search out the sources of the Arkansas and Red rivers. Then he was to follow each stream back to the American settlements. Long marched his men to the Rocky Mountains, where it was believed that the rivers began. Major Long reached the Rocky Mountains by traveling up the Missouri and Platte rivers into Colorado.

During July, 1820, the Long expedition reached the central Rocky Mountains. They found what they believed to be the source of the Arkansas River. Long ordered Captain John R. Bell and twelve men to follow the Arkansas River back to Fort Smith. Captain Bell's men suffered great hardship while riding along the Arkansas River. They crossed Colorado, Kansas, and Oklahoma in the scorching August heat and reached Fort Smith on September 9, 1820.

26.   Early-day photograph of the Great Salt Plains of Oklahoma.

Major Long led ten men southward through the Rocky Mountains. He searched for the headwaters of Red River. The explorers rode for five days across eastern New Mexico, until Long found a deep creek bed which he thought to be a tributary of Red River.

Unknown to him at the time, this creek bed was a tributary of the Canadian River, which flows through central Oklahoma. As Long's party crossed the plains, the stream bed they were following gradually widened. On September 10, 1820, Major Long and his men reached a point where what they thought was Red River joined a larger stream. It was then that Major Long realized his mistake. He had followed the Canadian River instead of the

43

27. Stephen H. Long, from a painting by C. W. Peale.

44

Red River. It was too late in the year to return to the plains and search out Red River. Therefore, the Long expedition continued along the larger stream, the Arkansas River. They reached Fort Smith on September 13, 1820.

The Nuttall Expedition—One other expedition into Oklahoma took place during this period. It produced valuable scientific information about Oklahoma. During 1819, Thomas Nuttall, a famous scientist, came to Fort Smith. He spent several months in eastern Oklahoma studying the geology, plants, and animals, and he collected many plants and rocks. Nuttall visited the land along the Grand, Verdigris, Cimarron, Poteau, and Arkansas rivers. He described his Oklahoma trip in a book titled *Journal of Travels in the Arkansas Territory*, one of the earliest scientific books on Oklahoma geology, plants, and animals.

These early explorations of Oklahoma were important because explorers prepared maps and wrote reports on the region. These maps and reports were published and people in the eastern United States were informed about Oklahoma. These explorations helped settle

28.   The countryside near Belle Point, from a landscape in *A Journal of Travel into the Arkansas Territory During the Year 1819,* by Thomas Nuttall.

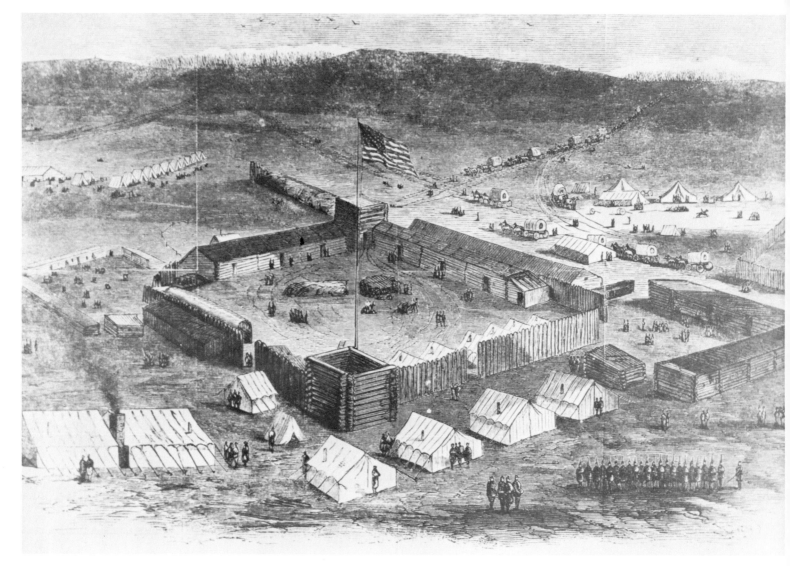

29. Camp Supply, Indian Territory, a typical log fort, as shown in *Harper's Weekly Magazine*, 1869.

30. Aerial view of the original Fort Gibson, restored from construction plans found in the National Archives.

the location of the boundary separating Spanish and American territory. Maps and reports prepared by explorers were important aids to American officials. In 1819 they signed the Adams-Onís Treaty. This agreement set the southern and western boundaries separating the territory of the United States and Spain. Portions of this boundary line—the Red River and the 100th meridian—later became the southern and western boundaries of the state of Oklahoma.

AMERICAN SOLDIERS IN OKLAHOMA

While Americans were exploring this region, the secretary of war was assigning soldiers to Oklahoma. Soldiers serving in Oklahoma had many duties. They were expected to protect the area against foreign invasion. Spain, the American neighbor in the Southwest, had been unfriendly to the United States for several years.

American Forts in Oklahoma—Soldiers were among the first American pioneers to reach Oklahoma. Soldiers assigned to the frontier had to be able to do many things. They had to have building skills because in the early days they built the forts. They went into the Oklahoma forests with sharp axes and felled large trees. They trimmed the trees into logs in order to form the high outer walls of a fort in the shape of a large square.

The outer log walls were called palisades. Each palisade log was twelve feet long and was sharpened to a point on the upper end. The pointed logs in the high walls made it difficult for an enemy to enter the fort. On each of the four corners of the fort, soldiers placed cannon, and they constructed a set of large entry gates in one wall. The gates opened to the outside and were locked on the inside. Inside the palisade walls soldiers built barracks, or living quarters, and storehouses for food and supplies. The log buildings included an armory for storing and repairing guns, and a magazine to store gunpowder.

American soldiers built several forts in Oklahoma. They established Fort Smith in 1817. It was situated on the Oklahoma-Arkansas border at the junction of the Arkansas and Poteau rivers. During 1824, soldiers erected Fort Gibson. It was situated near the mouth of Grand River in northeastern Oklahoma. And also in 1824, American troops erected Fort

48

Fort Koffee on the Arcansas river 15 m. above Fort Smith.
the 19 t of July 1853.

31.   Fort Coffee, on the Arkansas River fifteen miles above Fort Smith, sketched by H. B. Mollhausen, 1853.

32. "Artillery, Infantry, Dragoon (Full Dress), 1835–1850," a lithograph by H. A. Ogden in the *Army of the United States,* Washington, 1888.

Towson on Gates Creek near Red River in southeastern Oklahoma.

By 1861, soldiers constructed several other posts in Oklahoma. Camp Arbuckle, Camp Holmes, and Camp Washita were constructed in 1834 across central Oklahoma. That same year, soldiers erected Fort Coffee on the Arkansas River in eastern Oklahoma. In 1842, troops established Fort Washita in south-central Oklahoma. Fort Arbuckle, also situated in south-central Oklahoma, was completed in 1851. Eight years later, troops constructed Fort Cobb in southwestern Oklahoma.

Traders, trappers, and other pioneers collected around the Oklahoma forts. Merchants established stores near the forts. Towns grew up. Several towns near the old forts survive today, including Fort Gibson and Fort Cobb.

Soldiers as Pioneers—Soldiers were among the first American settlers in Oklahoma. Their mission was to guard the international boundary. They surveyed and mapped Oklahoma and built roads which connected the military posts with one another. Some roads linked the Oklahoma settlements with towns in Missouri, Arkansas, and Louisiana. Soldiers carried the first mail in this wilderness. They supervised trade with the Indian tribes. Soldiers watched for whisky and other illegal goods which some traders tried to bring into the Indian country. They guided the Eastern tribes to Oklahoma and protected them. Soldiers from Oklahoma forts also protected immigrants traveling in long trains of covered wagons across Oklahoma on their way to Texas and California.

Soldiers were among Oklahoma's first American farmers. In the early days soldiers had to raise most of their food. They cleared garden plots near the forts and planted corn, beans, potatoes, and other vegetables. They obtained most of their fresh meat by hunting for bear, deer, elk, and buffalo in the forests and on the prairies near the forts.

Many types of soldiers served in the Oklahoma forts. The first soldiers were infantry, foot soldiers, from the First Rifle Regiment. As the army changed its form, different types

33. Robert E. Lee as lieutenant of engineers.

34. War department
officials
inspecting
Fort Gibson,
1838.

of soldiers were assigned to the Oklahoma forts. These groups were cavalry, or mounted troops, engineers, and artillery.

In 1833 the United States Army formed its first cavalry unit at Fort Gibson. It was named the Dragoon Regiment. Troops for the Dragoon Regiment were recruited from New York, Cincinnati, and St. Louis. They were trained at Fort Gibson. The Dragoons wore flashy blue-and-gray uniforms. Each trooper wore a bright orange sash about his waist. Gold braid decorated his coat front and sleeves. He wore a tall hat topped with a white pompom. High black boots with spurs completed his uniform. He was mounted on a white horse. Each Dragoon's new rifle and saber flashed in the sunlight during drill periods.

Some of the leading men of the nation served as officers at the Oklahoma forts. They included Zachary Taylor, a general in the Mexican War and later president of the United States; Jefferson Davis, later United States secretary of war and president of the Confederate States of America; and Robert E. Lee, later commander in chief of Confederate armies in the Civil War.

PIONEER SETTLERS IN OKLAHOMA

American pioneers came to Oklahoma soon after it became United States territory in 1803. The settlers on the farms and in the towns prospered, as did the trappers and traders. Their successes attracted other pioneers. The population of early-day Oklahoma increased rather quickly.

The Long Knives—Soon after 1803, some restless, daring Americans entered Louisiana. They were called "Long Knives" on the frontier because each man carried a long, sharp skinning knife in his belt. Many Long Knives settled in Oklahoma because it was one of the most attractive portions of Louisiana. A rich trade in furs already had been established by French traders among the Osages, Quapaws, Wichitas, and other tribes. Oklahoma's waterways, centering on the Arkansas and Red rivers, were important. These river systems provided easy routes to New Orleans and other markets on the Gulf of Mexico.

Joseph Bogy and Pierre Chouteau were pioneer fur traders in Oklahoma. They established posts along the Grand and Verdigris

35. Jean Pierre Chouteau as he appeared about 1796.

54

rivers. And they formed a settlement at Three Forks, where the Verdigris, Grand, and Arkansas rivers merge. Their success attracted other traders.

By 1812 many American hunters, trappers, and traders had settled in eastern Oklahoma. They brought their families or formed families among the Indian nations. The trade towns at Three Forks supported fur-hunting expeditions into central and western Oklahoma.

Indian hunters brought to Three Forks their bales of beaver, bear, panther, wolf, and otter skins, their buffalo robes, elk and deer hides, and containers of bear oil. They exchanged these furs and hides for axes, knives, beads, cloth, guns, and ammunition. American trappers and hunters also came into Three Forks with their trains of pack horses loaded with furs and hides.

Pioneer settlers, too, came to Oklahoma soon after 1803. Tom Slover was an early-day settler on Grand River. He constructed a log home for his family on a high bluff near the river. Slover cleared fields in the forest and raised corn and other vegetables. He had herds of hogs, cattle, and horses. Mark Bean was a pioneer who settled in a log cabin on

36.   Salt works, Blaine County, Oklahoma Territory.

the Illinois River. Besides grain, he raised cattle, hogs, and poultry.

Frontiersmen also settled in southeastern Oklahoma near Red River. They cleared fields in the thick forests and planted grain. They raised cattle, horses, and hogs. Pioneer settlers in early-day Oklahoma also mined lead, refined salt, and gathered pecans, beeswax, and other products from nature.

The pioneers collected cargoes of their products at the landings on the Grand, Arkansas, and Red rivers. They shipped their products on flatboats to Gulf markets. Mark Bean, one of the leading Oklahoma pioneers, marketed grain and bacon, but salt was his most important export. On his farm was a salt spring. He placed the salt water from this spring in large iron vats. They were flat-shaped, like huge saucers. Heat from fires under the salt vats evaporated the water from the salt. Fifty-five gallons of salt water from Bean's salt spring produced a bushel of salt. Salt was one of the most valuable products produced on the Oklahoma frontier. At that time a bushel of salt sold for about five dollars.

The number of settlers in eastern Oklahoma increased. In 1824, Congress extended the western boundary of Arkansas Territory on a line through Fort Gibson to Red River. The Arkansas legislature created two large Arkansas counties in eastern Oklahoma. Lovely County was situated in the territory north of the Arkansas River. Its county seat was Nicksville, a log cabin settlement on the west bank of Sallisaw Creek. Miller County was situated in the territory extending from the Arkansas River south to Red River. Its county seat, situated near Red River, was named Miller's Courthouse.

Settlement of American pioneers in Oklahoma was stopped in 1825. The United States government changed the use of Oklahoma. American leaders decided to close Oklahoma to settlement by white pioneers, and to colonize Indian tribes from east of the Mississippi River in this land, which would be called Indian Territory. Those settlers on land in the Arkansas counties of eastern Oklahoma were required to move. During 1825 a north-south boundary line, running near Fort Smith from the Missouri border to Red River, was drawn. It separated Arkansas from Indian territory. Oklahoma's future was set. It was to be Indian Territory until 1906.

CHAPTER FOUR

The Indian Territory

Between 1830 and 1906, Oklahoma served the nation as the Indian Territory. The federal government resettled many tribes here from other parts of the United States. Indians came from the eastern United States. They came from the neighboring states of Kansas and Texas. And Indians from Arizona, California, Idaho, and Washington were settled in Oklahoma at this time.

The federal government relocated these tribes in Indian Territory to remove them from the path of American expansion. Settlers often desired land belonging to Indian tribes. In most cases, Indians were forced to give in to the wishes of the settlers.

PREPARING OKLAHOMA FOR INDIAN COLONIZATION

In the early years of Indian removal the tribal immigrants were from the eastern United States. Those tribes living in the territory south of the Ohio River were among the first to be colonized in Oklahoma. The Southern tribes were the Cherokees, Choctaws, Creeks, Seminoles, and Chickasaws. They owned rich agricultural land in Georgia, Florida, Alabama, and Mississippi.

Settlers wanted the land of the Southern tribes, and they urged government leaders to remove the Indians. Officials forced the Southern tribes to surrender their lands and move west to Indian Territory. Most leaders of the

Southern tribes were unwilling to do this. They loved the homeland where their people had lived for several centuries, and they did not wish to move west to Indian Territory.

Southern tribal leaders realized that the land in Indian Territory already belonged to other Indian tribes. Osages and Quapaws lived in eastern Oklahoma. Wichitas, Caddoes, Comanches, Kiowas, and Plains Apaches resided in western Oklahoma. The Oklahoma tribes did not wish to give up parts of their territories to make room for the Southern tribes.

Early Land Surrender Treaties—Federal officials worked to make the Indian Territory a safe place for the Southern tribes to settle. They urged the local tribes to surrender lands. After much pressure, government agents completed treaties with the Osages and Quapaws, who agreed to transfer their lands in Oklahoma. The Southern tribes could settle on these lands.

In 1818 and 1825 the Osages signed treaties giving up their claim to land in northern Oklahoma. By the 1825 treaty, the Osages agreed to move from Oklahoma, and to accept a reservation in southern Kansas. In 1818 the Quapaws gave up their land in Oklahoma. These treaties with the Osages and Quapaws opened the way for federal officials to relocate the Southern tribes in Indian Territory.

Federal officials had not discussed their plan to colonize eastern Indians with the Wichitas, Caddoes, Kiowas, Comanches, and Plains Apaches. These tribes had signed no treaties with the United States.

The Osages had signed treaties giving up their territory in Oklahoma, yet they remained on the land. They were determined not to move, and they warned that they would make war on intruders.

The Osages had fought many battles against the Cherokees. For several years Cherokees from Tennessee had been moving west of the Mississippi River. They settled in northwestern Arkansas, and roamed across Oklahoma searching for buffalo. Osage warriors attacked their villages. The Cherokees tired of these Osage raids. In 1817 a Cherokee army attacked an Osage village at Claremore's Mound in northeastern Oklahoma and defeated the Osages. They destroyed the village and took many women and children captives.

The Claremore Mound defeat raised Osage

fury and they raided the Cherokees. Federal officials faced a problem. The Southern tribes refused to surrender their eastern lands and move to Oklahoma until the Osages and other tribes were willing to receive them peacefully.

Peace on the Oklahoma Frontier—Federal officials were determined to move the Southern tribes to Oklahoma. Pioneers demanded their lands. President Andrew Jackson was concerned with white settlers and their wishes, but he was not concerned about justice for the Indians. He was determined to remove all Indians from the eastern United States. In 1830, Congress passed the Indian Removal Act, which increased the power of the federal government over Indians.

The War Department was expected to bring peace to the Indian Territory. The secretary of war assigned more troops at Fort Gibson and other Oklahoma military posts. The new troops included the Dragoons. The presence of more American soldiers in Oklahoma caused the Osages to end their raids on the Cherokees.

The tribes of western Oklahoma also were a problem. Federal officials decided to send the Dragoons to their country. During 1834, General Henry Leavenworth and Colonel Henry Dodge led the Dragoons on a long march to the Wichita Mountains in southwestern Oklahoma. They were to establish contact with the Wichitas, Caddoes, Comanches, Kiowas, and Plains Apaches. These Indians courteously received the Americans.

George Catlin was an artist from Philadelphia who accompanied the expedition and sketched these Indian people in their villages. Catlin wrote a book titled *North American Indians* which describes his adventures among these tribes.

After the Dragoon expedition, leaders of the western tribes met with federal officials and signed treaties with the United States. The western tribes promised to remain at peace with the United States. They agreed to allow travel across their lands, and they were willing to permit tribes from the eastern part of the country to settle in Oklahoma.

The Stokes Commission—President Jackson appointed three men to prepare the Indian Territory for the arrival of the Southern tribes.

37. Dragoon expedition meeting with the Comanches in the Wichita Mountains, 1834. From a sketch by George Catlin.

This group was named the Stokes Commission. Its chairman was Montfort Stokes, and the other members were Henry L. Ellsworth and John W. Schermerhorn. The Stokes Commission members traveled to Oklahoma and established their headquarters at Fort Gibson.

Several well-known persons accompanied the Stokes Commission to Indian Territory.

Among them was Washington Irving, America's best-known writer of the time. Irving hunted buffalo and chased wild horses on the prairies west of Fort Gibson. He described his adventures in the book *A Tour on the Prairies*.

The Stokes Commission first looked after a band of Seneca Indians from Ohio. Seneca leaders made a treaty granting their eastern lands to the United States. The Stokes Commission assigned the Senecas a small reservation in northeastern Oklahoma. Several Shawnee Indians joined the Senecas on their new reservation. When the Stokes Commission reached the Indian Territory, the Quapaws were living on Red River. The Stokes Commission assigned the Quapaws a reservation in northeastern Oklahoma next to the Senecas and Shawnees.

Dealing with the Osages was difficult. The Stokes Commission held several councils with Osage leaders. Commissioner Stokes urged the Osages to move to their reservation in southern Kansas but for a time the Osages refused. The large number of soldiers at Fort Gibson discouraged the Osages from raiding

38.   Portrait of Washington Irving.

61

Indian settlements, and during 1834 they moved to southern Kansas.

REMOVAL OF THE SOUTHERN TRIBES

Leaders of the Choctaws, Creeks, Cherokees, Seminoles, and Chickasaws saw that they would have to move their people to Oklahoma. Federal officials urged them to give up their eastern homelands. State officials in Georgia, Florida, Alabama, and Mississippi threatened to take over their lands. American pioneers trespassed on Indian property, and life became very difficult for the Southern Indians. Leaders of these tribes learned that the army and the Stokes Commission had made Oklahoma a safe place to settle their people.

The Choctaws—The Choctaws were the first Southern Indians to sign a removal treaty. The population of the Choctaw nation was about 22,000. Choctaw territory extended from central Mississippi to the Gulf of Mexico. The Choctaws were influenced by French, British, and Spanish traders. Europeans brought firearms, horses, cattle, hogs, and poultry to the Indians. Traders married Choctaw women,

39. Moshulatubbee, one of the Choctaw chiefs who signed an early removal treaty. From a painting by George Catlin, now in the Smithsonian Institution.

62

and soon there was a large group of mixed bloods in the Choctaw nation. Leflore, McCurtain, Folsom, McKenny, Jones, and Locke became common Choctaw family names.

Mixed-blood Choctaws became the leaders. They established plantations, farms, ranches, and businesses in the Choctaw nation. Many of them became slaveholders like their American neighbors. Full-blood Choctaws followed old tribal ways. In their simple life, close to nature, they lived in log cabins, farmed small patches of food crops, and spent much time hunting and fishing.

Missionaries from the Presbyterian, Baptist, and Methodist churches came to the Choctaw nation to establish schools for Choctaw children. Cyrus Kingsbury and Cyrus Byington were Presbyterian missionaries. They formed a system of writing the Choctaw language. Missionaries established small printing presses in the Choctaw nation and published textbooks and other reading material in the Choctaw language.

Soon after 1800, Choctaw leaders strengthened the tribal government by adopting a code of written laws. In 1826 they wrote a constitution for the tribal government.

Choctaw removal to Oklahoma began in 1820. Choctaw leaders and American agents signed the Treaty of Doak's Stand. The Choctaws agreed to cede to the United States a portion of their land in Mississippi in exchange for a large tract of land in Indian Territory. It was situated in the southern half of Oklahoma. Choctaw lands extended from the western border of Arkansas to the 100th meridian. The northern boundary of the Choctaw nation was formed by the Arkansas and Canadian rivers, the southern boundary, by the Red River.

Only about 1,000 Choctaws moved to Oklahoma by this treaty. Federal and state pressure increased on the Choctaws to give up all their eastern lands. In 1830, Choctaw leaders again met with American agents. They signed the Treaty of Dancing Rabbit Creek. It was the final Choctaw removal treaty. The Choctaws turned over to the United States all of their lands in Mississippi. Most of the Choctaws agreed to remove to the Indian Territory. They were to settle on the land assigned to them by the treaty of Doak's Stand.

The Creeks—The Creek nation extended over much of Alabama and western Georgia. They

63

numbered about 20,000. Like the Choctaws, the Creeks were influenced by French, Spanish, and British traders who came to live in their nation. They brought European weapons, tools, livestock, goods, and ways, and married Creek women. A large mixed-blood group developed in the Creek nation. McIntosh, Grayson, Stidham, and McGillivray became common family names.

The Creek nation was divided into two large groups. The Upper Creeks were mostly full bloods. They lived apart from the Lower Creeks. The Upper Creeks wished to preserve the Indian life style, close to nature. They supported themselves by farming, hunting, fishing, and trading. Opothleyaholo was the leader of the Upper Creeks.

Lower Creeks were mostly mixed bloods. The McIntosh family was the leader of this group. The mixed bloods became skilled in agriculture, stock raising, and business. They operated plantations, farms, and ranches, and many of them were slaveholders.

Like the other Southern tribes, the Creeks were urged to sign over their lands and move to Indian Territory. Finally in 1826, Creek leaders signed the First Treaty of Washington,

40. Opothleyaholo, Creek leader.

by which they gave up a large portion of their eastern lands. In return they received a new home in the center of Indian Territory. About one-fourth of the Creek nation moved to Oklahoma. Most of the early immigrants were mixed-blood Lower Creeks led by the McIntosh family.

The Upper Creeks were much more difficult to deal with. Federal and state officials urged all of the Creeks to move to Indian Territory. Settlers trespassed on their lands and stole their livestock. Life became so unpleasant that the Creeks agreed to move to Indian Territory. In 1832, Creek leaders signed the Second Treaty of Washington. It required the remainder of the Creek nation to remove to Indian Territory. They were to settle on lands assigned to the Creek nation by the First Treaty of Washington.

The Cherokees—The Cherokees numbered about 20,000. At one time their territory extended from North and South Carolina across Tennessee and Georgia. They had released much of this land to the United States. By the time of removal, all that remained of their eastern territory was a large tract of land in northwestern Georgia.

41.   John Ross, by John Neagle, 1846.

In colonial times the Cherokees came under the influence of British traders. The traders introduced firearms, trade goods, and livestock into the Cherokee nation. The Europeans married Cherokee women which gave rise to a large mixed-blood population. Common family names were Rogers, Ward, Adair, Vann, Chisholm, Ross, and Lowry. Mixed bloods became the leaders of the Cherokee nation. Many Cherokees were successful businessmen. Several tribal citizens established prosperous plantations, farms, and ranches, and a number of Cherokees were slaveowners.

The Cherokees adopted a written constitution in 1827. Their constitution created the office of principal chief, elected by the people. It provided for courts and a national council to make laws. John Ross was the first elected principal chief of the Cherokee nation.

Missionaries from the Presbyterian and Moravian churches established schools among the Cherokees. Sequoyah was a Cherokee silversmith. During the 1820's he invented the Cherokee syllabary, or alphabet. It converted the Cherokee spoken language to written form. Printing presses in the Cherokee nation published books and other reading materials

42. Sequoyah, inventor of the Cherokee alphabet.

in the Cherokee language. In 1828 the Cherokee government established the first newspaper published by an Indian tribe. It was named the *Cherokee Phoenix*. The editor published news in Cherokee and in English.

Georgia citizens wanted the Cherokees' land. They expected the Cherokees to give up their Georgia lands. Federal agents urged the Eastern Cherokees to join the Western Cherokees, who had lived west of the Mississippi River for nearly fifty years. In 1817 the federal government assigned the Western Cherokees a reservation in northwestern Arkansas. Nearly 5,000 Cherokees settled on this reservation. Soon Arkansas settlers demanded this land. In 1828 the federal government signed a treaty with the Western Cherokees. The Western Cherokees exchanged their land in Arkansas for a new home in Indian Territory. It covered the northern third of Oklahoma and was divided into two parts.

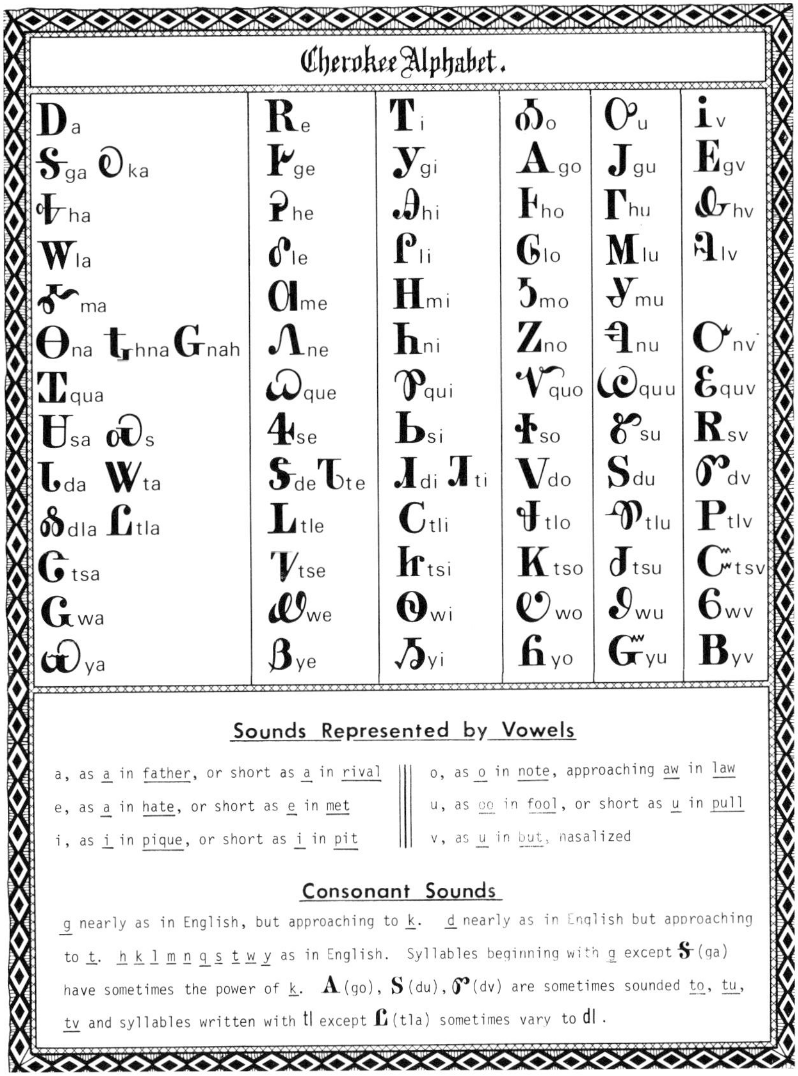

43. The Cherokee alphabet.
From *Beginning Cherokee,*
by Ruth Bradley Holmes and Betty Sharp Smith.

Cherokee Alphabet.

D a	R e	T i	Ꭳ o	Ꮏ u	i v
Ꮝ ga Ꮖ ka	Ꮅ ge	Ꮹ gi	A go	J gu	Ꭼ gv
Ꮀ ha	Ꮄ he	Ꭿ hi	Ꮁ ho	� hu	Ꭽ hv
W la	Ꮞ le	Ꮅ li	Ꮐ lo	M lu	Ꮑ lv
Ꮪ ma	Ꮷ me	H mi	Ꮏ mo	Ꮶ mu	
Ꮎ na Ꮏ hna Ꮎ nah	Ꮄ ne	Ꮒ ni	Z no	Ꮔ nu	Ꮕ nv
Ꮖ qua	Ꮗ que	Ꮙ qui	Ꮖ quo	Ꮖ quu	Ꮖ quv
Ꮜ sa Ꮝ s	Ꮞ se	Ꮟ si	Ꮢ so	Ꮥ su	Ꮡ sv
Ꮃ da Ꮙ ta	Ꮥ de Ꮦ te	Ꮧ di Ꮨ ti	V do	Ꮪ du	Ꮩ dv
Ꮪ dla Ꮃ tla	L tle	C tli	Ꮮ tlo	Ꮯ tlu	P tlv
Ꮳ tsa	Ꮴ tse	Ꮵ tsi	K tso	Ꮶ tsu	Ꮷ tsv
Ꮹ wa	Ꮺ we	Ꮻ wi	Ꮼ wo	Ꮽ wu	Ꮾ wv
Ꮿ ya	Ꭰ ye	Ꭱ yi	Ꭲ yo	Ꭳ yu	Ꭴ yv

Sounds Represented by Vowels

a, as a in <u>father</u>, or short as a in <u>rival</u>

e, as a in <u>hate</u>, or short as e in <u>met</u>

i, as i in <u>pique</u>, or short as i in <u>pit</u>

o, as o in <u>note</u>, approaching <u>aw</u> in <u>law</u>

u, as oo in <u>fool</u>, or short as u in <u>pull</u>

v, as u in <u>but</u>, nasalized

Consonant Sounds

g nearly as in English, but approaching to k. d nearly as in English but approaching to t. h k l m n q s t w y as in English. Syllables beginning with g except Ꮝ (ga) have sometimes the power of k. A (go), Ꮪ (du), Ꮩ (dv) are sometimes sounded to, tu, tv and syllables written with tl except Ꮮ (tla) sometimes vary to dl.

The territory between Grand River and the 96th meridian was the Cherokee nation, proper; the territory between the 96th meridian and the 100th meridian was called the Cherokee Outlet. Federal officials and Georgians expected the Eastern Cherokees to move to this land assigned to the Western Cherokees.

Georgia citizens and officials applied great pressure on the Eastern Cherokees. The Georgia legislature adopted laws which abolished tribal government. Cherokee citizens were made subject to state law, and it became illegal for Cherokee officials to perform their tribal government duties. Georgia officials imprisoned several missionary teachers working among the Cherokees because it was believed that missionaries encouraged the Cherokees to remain in Georgia.

A small group of Cherokee mixed bloods led by John Ridge, Major Ridge, Stand Watie, and Elias Boudinot decided that the Cherokees had best move to Indian Territory before they lost everything. In 1835 they signed the Treaty of New Echota, which required the Cherokees to surrender their Georgia lands, amounting to 8,000,000 acres. In payment they were to receive $5,000,000, or about

44. Major Ridge, Cherokee leader and signer of the Treaty of New Echota.

sixty-five cents an acre. The Eastern Chero-kees were to settle in Indian Territory on land already assigned to the Western Chero-kees. The Treaty of New Echota permitted the Cherokees three years to prepare for the move to Oklahoma.

The Seminoles—The Seminoles lived in Flor-ida and were closely related to the Creeks. At the time of removal the Seminoles numbered about 3,500. They did not come under Amer-ican control until after 1819, when the United States acquired Florida from Spain.

The Seminoles supported themselves by farming, hunting, fishing, and trading. They were town dwellers. Their tribal system of rule consisted of local town governments. Each town was headed by a local leader called the band chief. Some of the leading band chiefs at the time of removal were Alligator, Jumper, Coacoochee, and Micanopy. The Seminole nation was governed by a principal chief and a council chosen by the people.

After the United States acquired Florida, settlers poured into the new territory. They demanded that the federal government open the Seminoles' rich lands to settlement. Sev-eral treaties with the United States reduced

45.   Tukoseemathla, a Seminole chief.

69

Seminole tribal lands which satisfied the settlers only for a short time. Soon they demanded that the federal government remove the Seminoles from Florida. Pioneers claimed that Indians stole their slaves and livestock and were dangerous neighbors.

In 1832, Seminole leaders signed the Treaty of Payne's Landing. This agreement required the Seminoles to emigrate to Indian Territory after tribal leaders found a suitable home there. The Seminoles had three years to complete their move.

The following year Seminole leaders traveled to Indian Territory and searched for a new home for the tribe. Creek leaders invited the Seminoles to settle in their territory. In 1833, Seminole chiefs signed the Treaty of Fort Gibson. By its terms the Seminoles accepted a home in the Creek nation.

46. Micanopy, Seminole leader.
From *Indian Tribes of North America,*
by McKenney and Hall.

The Chickasaws—At the time of removal the Chickasaws numbered about 4,500. They lived in large villages and supported themselves by farming, hunting, and trading. The Chickasaws had controlled a large territory extending over western Tennessee and Kentucky, northwestern Alabama, and northern Mississippi. They had an advanced system of tribal government and native religion.

The Chickasaws stressed bravery and daring in battle. They were much feared by neighboring tribes because of their military power. Three times during the 1700's French armies tried to conquer the Chickasaws, but each time the Chickasaws defeated the French.

The Chickasaws were friendly with the British. British traders came to the Chickasaw nation from South Carolina and brought the Chickasaws firearms, livestock, and Euro-

47. Tishomingo, the last war chief of the Chickasaw nation.

pean ways. They married Chickasaw women, which produced a large mixed-blood population. Mixed bloods became the business and political leaders of the Chickasaw nation. They managed large farms and plantations and many of them were slaveholders.

Chickasaw life changed after the United States gained control of the lower Mississippi Valley. Settlers and government officials urged the Chickasaws to release their lands, and Chickasaw leaders signed several treaties giving up portions of their territory. By 1830, all that remained was their homeland in northern Mississippi and northwestern Alabama.

The Chickasaws finally agreed to remove to Indian Territory. In 1832 tribal leaders and American agents signed the Treaty of Pontotoc. The Chickasaws gave up their eastern lands and agreed to remove to Indian Territory when their leaders found a home there.

For several years Chickasaw leaders explored Indian Territory. The Choctaws invited the Chickasaws to join them in southern Oklahoma. In 1837, Chickasaw and Choctaw leaders signed the Treaty of Doaksville. This agreement permitted the Chickasaws to settle in the Choctaw nation.

The Trail of Tears—The government completed the removal of most of the Southern Indians to Oklahoma during the 1830's. The Indians endured great suffering. During the march to Indian Territory many Indians died. Their removal is called the "Trail of Tears." It is said that roads and trails to Indian Territory were marked by the tombstones of those who died along the way. All migrating Indians suffered. Poor government planning was to blame. Many Indians were on the trail in midwinter, when temperatures often were below freezing. They marched through deep snow and mud, and they had little, if any, shelter at night. Most migrating parties were able to travel only about five miles a day. There were few wagons for transporting the people. Only the young, the old and feeble, the sick, and the blind were permitted to ride in wagons. Most Indians walked all the way to Oklahoma. Cholera, smallpox, and measles epidemics took many lives. Each tribe lost about one-fourth of its population on the westward march. This is why the removal is called the Trail of Tears.

Blacks, as slaves of Southern Indians, were in the removal, too. They did much of the

48. The Trail of Tears, from a drawing by Dick West, Cheyenne artist.

heavy work on the trail. Slaves loaded freight wagons and cared for livestock. Black workers opened roads for the overland march. They arrived early in Oklahoma and they rank among the pioneer settlers of this area.

The Chickasaw and Choctaw removals were the most orderly. Yet members of these tribes lost livestock and other personal property along the way, and disease epidemics struck their removal parties, causing much suffering and many deaths.

The Cherokee, Creek, and Seminole removals were the most difficult. Many of these Indians were determined not to leave the land of their ancestors. The federal government sent soldiers into the Cherokee nation, Creek nation, and Seminole nation to drive these Indians to Oklahoma. Many Cherokees es-

73

caped the soldiers and hid in the mountains. Today a large group of Cherokees lives in the mountains of North Carolina. They are the descendants of those Indians who escaped the soldiers.

There was trouble in the Creek nation. Creeks gathered their livestock and other property and prepared to move to Oklahoma, but before they were ready, settlers invaded their Alabama lands. The Creeks defended their homes and drove off the settlers. The intruders asked for protection from the angry Indians and the federal government sent soldiers to the Creek nation to protect the settlers. Soldiers arrested many Creek warriors, placed the Indians in shackles and chains, and drove them with bayonets to Indian Territory.

The Seminoles had the bloodiest removal. Osceola was a young Seminole warrior who was determined not to surrender his Florida homeland to the settlers. Many Seminoles joined him. They promised to defend their homeland as Indian patriots, and they fought a long war of resistance against the United States Army.

During the Seminole War, Osceola was taken prisoner under a flag of truce. American officers sent him to military prison, believing that with Osceola out of the way, Seminole resistance to removal would end. They were mistaken, because Jumper and other leaders took his place and the war continued.

Finally, in 1842, the federal government gave up on the Seminoles. By this time about 3,000 Seminoles had been delivered to Indian Territory, but several hundred Seminoles hid in the Florida Everglades and escaped removal to Oklahoma. Their descendants live in Florida today.

Most of the Indians of the Southern tribes finally were settled in Oklahoma. They had lost many relatives and friends on the Trail of Tears. Their hearts were heavy. They had been driven from their homes in the east. They had lost livestock, farming implements, and other property on the march west. Yet they turned with courage to the task of making a fresh start in the Oklahoma wilderness.

CHAPTER FIVE

Land of Differing Indian Cultures

Most of the Southern Indians reached Oklahoma during the 1830's. After their arrival, Indian Territory became a mixture of different Indian cultures. In eastern Oklahoma lived the Choctaws, Cherokees, Creeks, Seminoles, and Chickasaws. They were called the Five Civilized Tribes. This was because they had adopted many European and American ways. Indians of the Five Civilized Tribes dressed like American pioneers. Many Cherokees, Choctaws, and other Southern Indians were well educated. They knew how to operate businesses, plantations, farms, and ranches. Many were slaveholders.

In western Oklahoma lived the Wichitas, Caddoes, Comanches, Kiowas, and Plains Apaches. Some of these western tribes were not like the Indians living in eastern Oklahoma. The Wichitas and Caddoes had adopted many European ways. Frenchmen had lived with them in earlier times, and they were farmers and traders. Their neighbors in western Oklahoma were the Comanches, Kiowas, and Plains Apaches. These Indians did no farming, but hunted the buffalo. Comanches and Kiowas were skilled horsemen and fierce fighters. They roamed over a wide territory and raided Spanish and Mexican settlements in Texas, New Mexico, and northern Mexico.

THE INDIANS OF
EASTERN OKLAHOMA

The 1830 map of Indian Territory divided Oklahoma into three Indian nations. The map showed the northern third of Oklahoma as the Cherokee nation. Central Oklahoma west of Fort Gibson was the Creek nation. Southern Oklahoma was the Choctaw nation. The tribal names on this map soon changed. In 1833 the Seminoles accepted a home with the Creeks. Then the map for central Oklahoma was changed to the Creek-Seminole nation. In 1837 the Chickasaws agreed to settle among the Choctaws. For a time the southern part of the map for Indian Territory was marked Choctaw-Chickasaw nation.

In a few years the map for Indian Territory had to be changed again. During 1855 the Chickasaws received a territory of their own in the center of the old Choctaw nation. The western third of the old Choctaw nation, situated between the 98th and 100th meridians, became the Leased District. This land was to be the home for the tribes of western Oklahoma.

During 1856 another map change was required. The Seminoles received a territory of their own in the western Creek nation. It was situated between the Canadian and North Canadian rivers. With these changes, after 1856 the number of Indian nations in Oklahoma increased from three to five. All of Oklahoma (except the Seneca, Shawnee, and Quapaw reservations in northeastern Oklahoma and the Panhandle) belonged to the Five Civilized Tribes.

Citizens of the Five Civilized Tribes settled in the territory assigned to them. Leaders of these Indian nations established governments, towns, schools, and businesses.

The Choctaws—The Choctaws were the first of the Five Civilized Tribes to accept a home in Oklahoma. Choctaw pioneers began to move to southern Oklahoma in 1820. Their early years in the Oklahoma wilderness were harsh. The Choctaws had lost much livestock and farming equipment during the removal. They were in poverty. The Choctaws first supported themselves by hunting, fishing, and trapping. They also gathered nuts, berries, herbs, and wild honey.

The Choctaws had a vast territory. By Indian law they held their lands in common, which meant that the land was owned by the

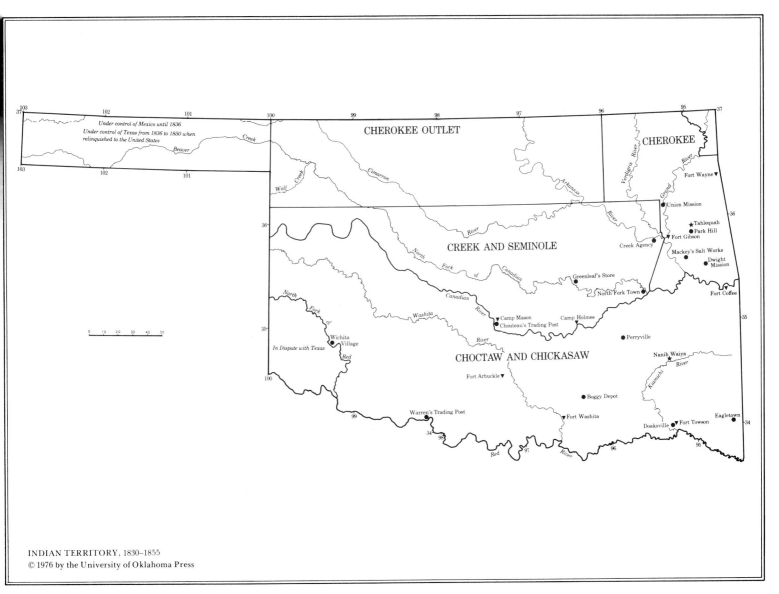

Indian Territory, 1830–1855

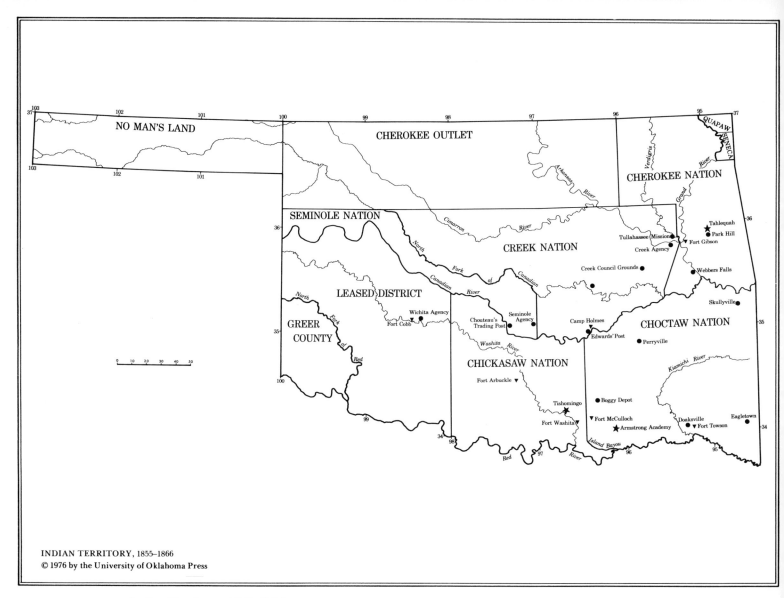

Indian Territory, 1855–1866

tribe. All members of the tribe had equal rights to share in the use of tribal lands.

Choctaw pioneers cleared fields and planted crops. Many Choctaws had slaves who worked with them in opening the Oklahoma wilderness. They hewed logs from trees in the forest and constructed cabins. Some were single-room cabins. Others were double log cabins, connected by a passageway called a dog trot. Back of their cabins Choctaw pioneers built log stables, barns, and corrals. Later many Choctaws replaced their log cabins with large frame and stone houses.

Full-blood Choctaws had simple tastes and needs. They cleared garden patches in the forest and raised corn, beans, and other food crops. Full bloods hunted, fished, and traded furs. They also raised small herds of cattle and horses.

Mixed bloods generally cleared larger farms. Several Choctaws operated huge plantations in the Red River valley. Their slaves cultivated fields of cotton and corn. Robert M. Jones, a Choctaw planter, was one of the wealthiest men in the West. He owned five hundred slaves who worked his five Red River plantations. Jones also owned a fleet of river

steamers. His boats ran between Kiamichi Landing on Red River and New Orleans.

Soon after they arrived in Oklahoma, the Choctaws established a tribal government. In 1834, Choctaw leaders met at Nanih Waiya, a Choctaw town on the Kiamichi River. They drafted the first constitution to be written in Oklahoma.

The Choctaw constitution formed a tribal government. It divided the Choctaw nation into three districts. Choctaw voters elected the principal chief and members of the national council. The Choctaw constitution contained a bill of rights which included trial by jury. Male Choctaw citizens twenty-one years of age or older could vote. The Choctaw council adopted several important laws. One law created the light horse, a body of mounted law enforcement officers. They patrolled the Choctaw nation and maintained peace and order. Choctaw leaders at this time were Nitakechi, Moshulatubbee, Joseph Kincaid, and Joseph Harkins. Each served the Choctaw nation as principal chief.

The Choctaws established a school system. Some were public schools, supported by tribal funds. Other schools were established by

79

49. Choctaw Council House built in 1834 at Nanih Waiya, near Tuskahoma.

50. Choctaw Female Seminary, Tuskahoma.

51.   Jones Academy in the Choctaw nation.

Presbyterian and Baptist missionaries. Schools in the Choctaw nation included Wheelock, Stockbridge, Goodwater, and Spencer Academy. Graduates from Choctaw nation schools studied at colleges in the eastern United States.

Cyrus Kingsbury and Cyrus Byington were Presbyterian missionaries who had worked among the Choctaws in the East. They joined the Choctaws in Indian Territory. Alfred Wright was another Presbyterian missionary working among the Choctaws. Alexander Talley was a Methodist missionary to the Choctaws. Isaac McCoy and Joseph Murrow were Baptist missionaries assigned to the Choctaw nation.

The Cherokees—The Eastern Cherokees suffered great hardships on their Trail of Tears to Oklahoma. The Western Cherokees welcomed the Eastern Cherokees and shared their food and homes until the newcomers could make a fresh start. Cherokee immigrants had lost most of their livestock and property during the removal. With the help of slave labor they established farms, plantations, and ranches. Cherokee farmers produced corn, wheat, and other small grains. They developed large herds of both cattle and horses.

Many salt springs were situated in the Cherokee nation. Indians opened salt works at these springs. Each year they exported several tons of salt. Cherokee farmers also exported meat and grain cargoes to New Orleans.

The nearby military posts—Fort Smith, Fort Gibson, and Fort Coffee—were important markets for Cherokee products. The secretary of war changed the policy of requiring soldiers to raise their food. Officers at the Oklahoma forts purchased vegetables, meat, and grain to feed the troops and the cavalry horses. Cherokee farmers supplied many of these needs.

Soon after the Eastern Cherokees reached Oklahoma they established a new government. The Western Cherokees already had a government and they invited the Eastern Cherokees to become a part of it. But the Eastern Cherokees were led by Chief John Ross, who believed that the re-united Cherokee nation should follow the government of the Eastern Cherokees. He had more followers than the Western Cherokees. Therefore, Ross won out

52. Rose Cottage, home of Chief John Ross at Park Hill. From *The Five Civilized Tribes,* by Grant Foreman.

53.　Cherokee Male Seminary, Tahlequah.

54. Cherokee Female Seminary, Tahlequah.

over the objections of the Western Cherokees.

Ross called a convention to meet at Tahlequah on September 6, 1839. The convention members wrote a constitution for the re-united Cherokee nation. This constitution guided the Cherokee nation until Oklahoma statehood in 1907.

The Cherokee constitution of 1839 provided for a principal chief. It created a law-making body called the national council, and a judicial branch. The Cherokee constitution contained a bill of rights. Male Cherokee citizens eighteen years of age or over could vote. They elected the principal chief and council members. Tahlequah became the capital of the Cherokee nation. John Ross was elected principal chief in the first election held under this constitution. He was re-elected to that office until his death in 1866.

There were two types of schools in the Cherokee nation, private schools run by missionaries, and public schools supported by tribal funds. The Cherokee public school system extended from kindergarten through grammar school, or eighth grade, to seminary, or high school, level. The Cherokee male and female seminaries were located near Tahlequah. Tribal scholarships permitted Cherokee students to continue their studies at Yale, Dartmouth, and other eastern colleges and universities.

Missionaries to the Indians were supported by eastern churches. They continued to work among the Cherokees after they arrived in Oklahoma. Samuel A. Worcester was the most famous missionary teacher. He had worked among the Cherokees while they were in Georgia. Worcester came over the Cherokee Trail of Tears, settled near Tahlequah, and established the town of Park Hill. It became famous over the Southwest as a center of learning. At Park Hill, Worcester founded a school and a church. He imported a printing press and type from the eastern United States. On the Park Hill Press Worcester published the *Cherokee Almanac*, *Cherokee Primer*, and other books in Cherokee and English.

Moravian and Baptist missionaries also worked among the Cherokees. Evan Jones was the best known of the Baptist missionaries. He also imported a printing press and type from the eastern United States and founded Baptist Mission Press. There he printed religious material and hymn books for the Cherokees and published the *Cherokee Messenger*. This was Oklahoma's first magazine. It contained tribal and religious news.

The Creeks—The Lower Creeks, led by the McIntosh family, were the first pioneers of this tribe to settle the Oklahoma wilderness. Beginning in 1826 they settled west of Fort Gibson. After 1832 the Upper Creeks, led by Opothleyaholo, arrived in Indian Territory. The Upper Creeks settled apart from the Lower Creeks. Most of their homes were situated near Little River.

Creek pioneers farmed, raised livestock, hunted, and traded with the Plains tribes of western Oklahoma. Prosperous mixed-blood Creek planters included Benjamin Perryman and Roley McIntosh. They established large plantations in the fertile Canadian River valley. Most of the labor on the Creek plantations was performed by slaves.

Creek planters raised cotton and corn. They transported their products to Gulf markets on steamers. These river boats ran between Fort Gibson Landing and New Orleans.

The Upper Creek settlements along Little

55. Samuel Austin Worcester, missionary to the Cherokees.

River were populated by full-blood Indians. They farmed small plots of corn, beans, and other vegetables. They also raised some cattle and horses. Upper Creeks hunted deer and wild turkey and trapped fur-bearing animals. They traded their furs for gunpowder, lead, salt, and blankets.

After the Creeks reached Oklahoma they continued the tribal government which they had used in the East. The Creek nation was divided into the Upper Creeks and the Lower Creeks. The Upper Creeks were led by Opothleyaholo. Roley McIntosh was the leader of the Lower Creeks at the time of their arrival in Indian Territory, and members of the McIntosh family continued to lead them.

The two divisions of the Creek nation were divided into towns. Each town had its chief and council, composed of leading warriors. Every year the Upper and Lower Creek chiefs and the council met at the national capital to conduct the business of the Creek nation. The council adopted laws.

The Seminoles were a part of the Creek nation after 1833, and they were subject to Creek law. Seminole leaders wished to have a separate nation. They urged the Creeks to permit them to settle in a territory of their own, but the Creeks did not agree to this until 1856.

In 1859, Creek leaders drafted a constitution which contained a bill of rights. Male tribal citizens eighteen years of age and older could vote. They were to elect a national council which would be the Creek law-making body. They were to elect two principal chiefs, one each for the Upper and Lower Creek tribal divisions.

In the first election under this constitution, Motey Kinnard was elected chief of the Lower Creeks. Echo Harjo was elected chief of the Upper Creeks. The capital of the Creek nation was first situated at Council Hill, near present Muskogee. The large capitol building was constructed of logs.

The Creeks were interested in educating their young people. Missionaries served as teachers in Creek nation schools. Each year the Creek council granted tribal funds to support the mission schools. William S. Robertson, a Presbyterian missionary, was a teacher among the Creeks who prepared textbooks in

56. Tullahassee Mission, Creek nation.

the Creek language. He established several schools in the Creek nation, including Tulla-hassee.

Methodist missionaries also labored in the Creek nation. Thomas B. Ruble was a Methodist missionary to the Creeks. In 1850 he established Asbury Manual Labor School, near North Fork Town.

The Seminoles—In Florida many Seminole warriors had fought a long, bloody war against the United States Army. They were opposed to moving to Indian Territory. The Seminole removal to Oklahoma was slow and troubled. Many Seminoles came to Oklahoma under military guard. They suffered heavy loss of life and property.

The Seminoles were a proud and independent people. They were unhappy because they had to live among the Creeks and were subject to Creek law. Seminoles wanted a territory of their own, where they could establish their government separate from the Creeks. But for several years the Creeks refused to grant their wish.

Coacoochee was a Seminole war chief. He had been a leader in the war in Florida against the United States. He was unhappy at having to live in the Creek nation. Soon after he arrived in Indian Territory, Coacoochee led several hundred Seminoles and their slaves to Mexico. The Mexican government granted the Seminoles a tract of land in the north Mexican state of Coahuila. After a time, some of the Seminoles returned to Indian Territory. However, many remained. Their descendants reside in northern Mexico today.

Seminoles continued to plead with the Creeks to allow them to settle in a separate territory under their own government. Finally, in 1856, the Creeks consented. The Seminoles were assigned a territory in western Oklahoma, between the North Canadian and Canadian rivers west of the 97th meridian.

The Seminoles moved at once into their new country. They established their capital near present Wanette. Seminoles settled in twenty-five small towns. Each town was governed by a chief and council of warriors. Each year the town chiefs and leading warriors of the nation gathered at the national capital to meet with the principal chief to conduct the business of the Seminole nation.

Seminoles supported themselves by farming,

hunting, and trading. Seminole stockmen grazed small herds of cattle and horses on the grasslands of their domain. They hunted buffalo, trapped fur-bearing animals, and traded with the tribes of western Oklahoma.

The Seminoles supported education for their young people. John Bemo, a nephew of Osceola, was a leading teacher. Presbyterians in the eastern United States supported Bemo's work. He founded schools among the Seminoles in Oklahoma. One school was Oak Ridge Mission, located near present Holdenville. John Lilley and James R. Ramsey were Presbyterian missionaries who worked with Bemo among the Seminoles.

The Chickasaws—By the Treaty of Doaksville in 1837 the Chickasaws agreed to settle in the Choctaw nation in southern Oklahoma. The Chickasaws were a proud people who valued their freedom. They soon tired of living with the Choctaws.

During the 1840's Chickasaw leaders urged separation from the Choctaws. They wanted a separate territory where they could establish a tribal government. Finally, in 1855, Choctaw and Chickasaw leaders signed a treaty of separation. The Chickasaws received their own territory west of the Choctaw nation in south-central Oklahoma.

The year after separation from the Choctaws, Chickasaw leaders wrote a constitution. It provided for a principal chief called the governor. Laws for the Chickasaws were to be made by the council. The constitution also created a system of courts. Male citizens nineteen years of age and older elected the governor and council members. Cyrus Harris was the first governor of the Chickasaw nation. The Chickasaw capital was located at Tishomingo.

Chickasaw settlers in the Oklahoma wilderness supported themselves in several ways. Many became ranchers. They raised fine horses and cattle on the grasslands of their territory. Chickasaw planters with slave labor opened huge plantations along the Red River and the Washita River. Their principal crops were cotton and corn. Robert Love, a Chickasaw mixed blood, owned 200 slaves. He operated two large plantations on Red River. Each autumn he chartered a river steamer to carry his cotton crop to New Orleans. Chickasaw farmers produced grain and vegetables for

92

57.   Third Chickasaw Capitol at Tishomingo.

58.   Bloomfield Academy for Chickasaw girls.

59. Students at Bloomfield Academy for Chickasaw girls, about 1900.

local markets at Fort Washita, Fort Arbuckle, and Fort Towson. Chickasaws traded with the Plains tribes and they operated ferries which transported passengers and wagons across Red River.

At first Chickasaw children attended Choctaw schools. After they formed a separate nation, the Chickasaws established neighborhood schools. Missionaries also established several schools for the Chickasaws. Wesley Browning was a Methodist educator and a pioneer teacher in the Chickasaw nation. Presbyterian missionaries worked among the Chickasaws, too. Advanced schools in the Chickasaw nation included the Chickasaw Academy, Bloomfield, and Wapanucka Institute.

Indian citizens of the Five Civilized Tribes established a new life in the Oklahoma wilderness. They recovered from the ruin of their Trail of Tears. They founded governments guided by constitutions. These Indian pioneers cleared forests and opened farms, plantations, and ranches, and they established towns, schools, and other improvements.

96

THE INDIANS OF WESTERN OKLAHOMA

In western Oklahoma lived the Plains tribes. They were different from the tribes of eastern Oklahoma. They had lived in Oklahoma longer than their eastern neighbors. Some were farmers who lived in villages near Red River, while others were migratory buffalo hunters. The Indians of western Oklahoma had no constitutional governments, schools, missionaries, or teachers. Their life style was much simpler than that of their eastern neighbors.

The Agricultural Tribes of Western Oklahoma — The oldest tribes of Oklahoma were the Wichitas and Caddoes. In earlier times they had lived in northern and eastern Oklahoma. Osages invaded this territory and forced them to move. They settled in southwestern Oklahoma near the Wichita Mountains.

Wichitas and Caddoes were skilled farmers. They lived in villages of dome-shaped houses covered with grass mats. They raised corn, beans, pumpkins, melons, and squash.

Many years before, the Wichitas and Caddoes had been in close contact with French

60. Kiowa infant in cradle board.

traders. They had learned to use European tools and firearms. Frenchmen hired Wichitas and Caddoes to trade with the Comanches and Kiowas, and they became skilled in frontier commerce. Many Wichitas and Caddoes spoke the French language. Later they learned the English language from American traders who came to their villages.

Wichita and Caddo traders traveled over the Southwest. They were well acquainted with the land, and often they were useful guides and interpreters for American exploring parties. The Wichitas and Caddoes were peaceful and cooperative with the Americans.

The Buffalo Hunting Tribes of Western Oklahoma—The Comanches, Kiowas, and Plains Apaches shared western Oklahoma with the Wichitas and Caddoes. They were skilled horsemen and hunters, who preferred the wandering life of hunting buffalo to farming. Each year they spent a season in the Wichita Mountains. The remainder of the year they ranged over a vast territory which extended from the Arkansas River southward to the Río Grande.

Comanches and Kiowas traveled in small

61. Wichita grass house, about 1870.

62.   Cheyenne-Arapaho encampment near Fort Reno.

63. Cheyenne village, with windbreaks.

bands. Each had fifty to three hundred Indians. Their houses were tipis. The tipi was a cone-shaped shelter, formed by long poles and covered with several sewed buffalo hides. It could be put up or taken down quickly like a tent. Each family carried the tipi and other household goods on a travois. The travois was made by strapping two long poles to the sides of a horse. Goods were packed on a platform near the end of the travois poles.

When Indian scouts located a buffalo herd, the hunting band stopped. Women and children busily set up camp. Some family members removed the poles and buffalo-hide covers from the travois and pitched the tipi. Others gathered wood and carried water to the campsite.

Indian hunters dismounted their slower-moving trail horses and selected from their horse herds the swiftest animals. Each hunter was armed with a sharp lance and bow and arrows. He daringly rode into the milling buffalo, selected his prey, then drove his lance or arrows deep into the heart of the huge, hairy beast. In a matter of minutes several dead animals littered the plains. Quickly the buffalo herd ran away to safety.

After the kill, the women came out. Their work was important, for the buffalo provided food, shelter, and clothing for the Indians. With sharp knives they carefully removed each hide. They would give special care to the hides in curing. From the buffalo hides they would make covers for the tipi. Buffalo hides also provided leather for footwear, belts and other clothing, and large bags for storing food. The women carved the meat from the carcass. Delicacies were the tongue, ribs, and hump. These they prepared for a feast that evening. The rest of the meat they cut into strips for drying in the sun. Dried buffalo meat kept for long periods and it was very nutritious. The women cleaned and washed the intestines, which, with the ends tied, were used like canteens to carry water. Even the bones were dried and used for tools.

Indian Wars in Western Oklahoma—Before the Civil War several battles were fought in western Oklahoma between Americans and Plains Indians. The Plains tribes resented expanding American settlements. Travel by Americans was increasing over their hunting range. The Indians claimed that this dis-

101

64. "The Buffalo Hunt," a painting by John Mix Stanley.

turbed the buffalo, causing them to become scarce. Their source of food, shelter, and clothing was threatened.

Several roads across Oklahoma connected the eastern United States with towns in the Southwest. One of these highways was the Texas Road, which crossed eastern Oklahoma into Texas and was used by thousands of settlers moving south. The Texas Road did not cross the Plains tribes' buffalo hunting range, but it did transport people into central Texas. Their settlements there threatened buffalo hunting by the Indians.

Several other roads crossed Oklahoma in an east-to-west direction. These roads affected the buffalo hunting range. One was the Butterfield Overland Stage and Mail Road. It ran from Fort Smith across the Choctaw and Chickasaw nations into Texas. The Butterfield Road continued to El Paso, Texas, and San Diego, California.

A traders' road ran from Fort Smith along the valley of the Canadian River into New Mexico. Each year caravans of freight wagons bound for Santa Fe moved over this highway. In 1849 troops from Fort Gibson laid out a road across central Oklahoma. This one was called the California Road. It was for the gold seekers. Each year several thousand travelers passed over the California Road on their way to the Pacific Coast.

Warriors from the Plains tribes raided overland caravans using the Oklahoma roads. Federal officials planned to protect the overland traffic. They decided to settle the Plains tribes on a reservation in western Oklahoma.

During 1855 federal officials signed an agreement with the Choctaws and Chickasaws. It permitted them to use the land between the 98th and 100th meridians as a reservation called the Leased District. The northern boundary was the Canadian River, and the southern boundary was the Red River.

Government agents settled 1,500 Indians in the Leased District. They were members of the Texas tribes—Wacos, Tonkawas, Anadarkos, Tawakonis, Ionis, and Keechies. Wichita Agency, near present Anadarko, supervised the Texas Indians. Fort Cobb was constructed in the Leased District during 1859 to protect these tribes.

The buffalo-hunting Comanches and Kiowas refused to accept a reservation in the Leased District. This caused the federal gov-

65.   A stagecoach providing passenger and mail service for Indian Territory.

66. Freight line serving Indian Territory settlements before the coming of railroads.

67.   Oxen-drawn freight wagons in Oklahoma City, 1889.

ernment and the state government of Texas to send troops against them. Officials planned to force these tribes to settle down and remain in the Leased District.

During 1858 a party of Texas Rangers led by Captain John Ford invaded the Leased District and fought several battles against the Comanches. And in 1858 a United States cavalry force commanded by Major Earl Van Dorn searched for Comanches and Kiowas. On October 1, 1858, Van Dorn's troopers found a Comanche village situated at Rush Springs in the southeastern corner of the Leased District. Van Dorn's men made a surprise attack. The Battle of Rush Springs destroyed this band of Comanches.

At that time the federal government failed to force the Plains tribes to remain on the Leased District reservation, because the Civil War broke out. The Civil War delayed the conquest of these tribes for nearly fifteen years.

CHAPTER SIX

Civil War and Reconstruction

In 1861 eleven southern states withdrew from the United States. This separation from the Union, or United States, was called secession. Slavery was practiced in all of the seceding southern states, and southern leaders feared that the federal government would abolish slavery. They formed a new nation from these eleven southern states. They called it the Confederate States of America. Jefferson Davis of Mississippi was elected president.

Abraham Lincoln, president of the United States, believed it was his duty to preserve the Union. He believed secession was unlawful, and he planned to use the army to destroy the Confederate States of America. He hoped to force the southern states to return to the Union. Confederate leaders were determined to remain separate from the United States. They raised an army to defend their territory from invasion by Union troops. There followed a bloody war, which lasted until 1865. It is called the Civil War.

Oklahoma became involved in the Civil War. Much fighting between Union and Confederate armies took place in Oklahoma. The Civil War weakened the Indian tribes of Oklahoma. It caused destruction and ruin.

BACKGROUND OF THE CIVIL WAR IN OKLAHOMA

In 1861, Indian Territory was prosperous. Oklahoma Indians had tamed the wilderness.

They had established farms, plantations, and ranches and had formed businesses. Their towns were busy commercial centers. They had a transportation system. Roads, ferries, and river steamers connected Oklahoma with towns in the East and the South. Tribal leaders had created governments based on written constitutions. The success and prosperity of the Five Civilized Tribes made their nations attractive to the Confederate States of America.

Confederate Interest in Oklahoma—Leaders of the Confederate States of America were interested in Indian Territory. Southerners had what is called the one-crop system. They raised either cotton, tobacco, or rice. They imported most of their food and other necessary goods.

When the Civil War broke out in 1861, Southerners lost their source of meat and grain in the northern United States. The Union government used the navy to blockade southern ports. This closed the Confederacy to shipping from Europe. The South had to look to the West for food and other goods.

Confederate leaders saw that Indian Territory could supply many of their needs. Oklahoma had vast cattle and horse herds. Indian farmers produced much grain. Oklahoma could furnish the Confederacy beef and flour. The lead and salt deposits of northeastern Indian Territory were very desirable to Confederate leaders.

Indian Territory's location was important for the Confederacy. It could connect the Confederacy with the far western territories. Confederate leaders hoped to bring New Mexico, Arizona, and California into the Confederacy. Confederate troops could move across Indian Territory to the west. Kansas, a Union state, was situated on Indian Territory's northern border. Texas, a Confederate state, was situated on Oklahoma's southern border. Oklahoma could protect Texas against Union invasion from Kansas. And Confederate armies from Oklahoma could invade Kansas.

Indian Interest in the Confederacy—Many Indians in the Five Civilized Tribes were slaveholders. They knew that President Lincoln wished to abolish slavery. To end slavery would cause severe loss to them. They had invested much wealth in slaves. In 1861 a slave was valued at about $1,200. There were over 5,000 slaves in Indian Territory. Many Indian citizens favored the Confederacy because that government would protect slavery.

Another reason many Oklahoma Indians favored the Confederacy was the threat to their land. The federal government had only recently taken their land in the eastern United States from them. That same government had forced them to remove to Indian Territory. Now leaders in the Union government promised the people of the northern United States that they would take the land of the Five Civilized Tribes in Oklahoma and open it to settlement. Fear for the safety of their lands was one of the strongest reasons for Indian interest in the Confederacy. Confederate leaders promised to protect the Indians of Oklahoma in their lands.

The Confederate Treaties—The Confederate capital was at Richmond, Virginia. Confederate officials there selected Albert Pike as commissioner to deal with the Indians of Oklahoma. Pike was an Arkansas lawyer and newspaper editor. He arrived in Indian Territory during the spring of 1861 to confer with the leaders of the Five Civilized Tribes. He signed a Confederate treaty of alliance with each of the Five Civilized Tribes. The Cherokee nation was the last tribe to sign, and leaders of this tribe completed their treaty with Pike during October, 1861. Pike also traveled to western Oklahoma. He met with the tribes of the Leased District at Wichita Agency. Wichitas, Caddoes, and other tribes signed Confederate treaties.

The Confederate government promised to guard and protect the Indian lands in Oklahoma. Each Indian nation was to raise an army to defend Oklahoma. The Confederate government was to arm and supply these Indian armies. But supplies were scarce in the south. Therefore, most of the Indian troops in Oklahoma were supplied and equipped by their tribal governments.

Oklahoma became a Confederate territory. It was placed in the Trans-Mississippi Department of the Confederate army. General Ben McCulloch of Texas was named to command the Indian troops. He also commanded the white troops raised in Arkansas, Louisiana, and Texas who served in Oklahoma. These Confederate troops were to guard the south-

68. General Douglas H. Cooper, commander of
Confederate Indian troops in the Civil War.

69. Colonel Tandy Walker, Choctaw-Chickasaw
Confederate brigade commander
in the Civil War.

70.   Stand Watie.

western border. Indian troops were assigned to Fort Smith, Fort Coffee, Fort Washita, Fort Arbuckle, Fort Towson, and Fort Cobb.

The Indian governments of Oklahoma raised four regiments of troops. One regiment consisted of Choctaws and Chickasaws. Douglas H. Cooper and Tandy Walker commanded this regiment. Creek and Seminole soldiers formed a second regiment. Chilly McIntosh, Creek leader, and John Jumper, Seminole chief, commanded this regiment. The Cherokees raised two regiments. One Cherokee regiment, composed of mixed bloods, was commanded by Stand Watie. It was called the First Cherokee Mounted Rifles. The other Cherokee regiment, commanded by John Drew, was made up of full bloods. It was called the Second Cherokee Regiment.

The four Indian regiments numbered about 5,000 men. Most of them were organized as cavalry. They were supported by Louisiana, Arkansas, and Texas troops from McCulloch's border army.

CIVIL WAR BATTLES IN OKLAHOMA

Several bloody battles were fought in Oklahoma during the Civil War. Union and Confederate armies marched across the Indian Territory several times. Often they met in combat. Their frequent battles caused many deaths. Both Union and Confederate troops burned houses, barns, and towns. They destroyed much property during these battles. By 1865, when the war ended, Oklahoma was a wasteland. The first blood shed on Oklahoma soil during the Civil War was caused by battles between Confederate Indians and neutral Indians.

Battles with Neutral Indians—Not all Oklahoma Indians favored the Confederacy. Several thousand Creeks, Seminoles, and Cherokees wished to remain neutral. They did not want to support either the Confederate or Union cause. They wanted to stay out of the Civil War altogether. Opothleyaholo, the Upper Creek chief, was the leader of this group. About 7,000 neutral Creek, Seminole, and Cherokee men, women, and children joined Opothleyaholo. They searched for a place where they would be safe from attack by Confederate troops.

Opothleyaholo led the neutral Indians to Round Mountain, near the mouth of the Cimarron River. Confederate scouts discovered Opothleyaholo's camp and informed Colonel Cooper. On November 19, 1861, Cooper, with 1,400 Confederate Indian cavalry, attacked Opothleyaholo's camp at Round Mountain. The neutral Indians bravely defended their families. They forced the Confederates to retreat. The Battle of Round Mountain was the first battle of the Civil War in Oklahoma.

Opothleyaholo quickly led his followers to a place farther away from the Confederate Indians. He stopped on Bird Creek at Chusto Talasah or Caving Banks, north of the Creek settlement of Tulsey Town (Tulsa). Cooper's scouts found Opothleyaholo's hiding place, and the Confederate Indian army struck the neutral Indians again. For the second time Opothleyaholo's warriors defeated them.

Opothleyaholo moved his followers a third time to a place called Chustenalah, on the eastern edge of the Cherokee Outlet. Cooper returned to Fort Gibson and prepared for a third attack against the neutral Indians. On December 26, 1861, his scouts located Opothleyaholo's camp at Chustenalah. Confederate troops surrounded the neutral Indians and attacked. The neutral Indians fought bravely

113

as before, but early in the battle they ran out of ammunition. Then the Confederate troops swept through their camp, and captured the wagons, equipment, and livestock. Opothleyaholo's people fled into the timber. On the night after the battle a fierce snowstorm struck. The cold weather caused great suffering. After the Confederate Indians withdrew, Opothleyaholo's people gathered from their hiding places and began the cold march to nearby Kansas. The Confederate victory at Chustenalah brought to a close the first year of the Civil War in Oklahoma.

Union Conquest of Oklahoma—Union commanders were determined to conquer Indian Territory. During 1862 and 1863 they sent several armies into Oklahoma to drive out the Confederates. In these Union armies were several hundred Creek, Seminole, and Cherokee soldiers, the former neutral Indians. The Union Indians were anxious to defeat the Confederate Indians and recover their homes in Oklahoma.

On March 6, 1862, a large Union army from Kansas marched southward along the Oklahoma-Arkansas border. Confederate armies in Indian Territory and Arkansas rushed north. They intended to drive the invaders back into Missouri and Kansas. Cherokee troops led by Colonel Stand Watie were a part of the Confederate force. The Union and Confederate armies met at Pea Ridge. This was at the tiny settlement of Elkhorn Tavern, near the western border of Arkansas. The bloody battle of Pea Ridge lasted two days. The Union army won the battle. Federal troops captured many Confederate soldiers and large amounts of arms and supplies. Watie's Cherokee cavalry fought bravely. His men captured a Union artillery battery, held their position on the Confederate line, and helped cover the Confederate retreat. They were among the last of the Rebel troops to leave the battlefield.

Soon Indian Territory faced another Union invasion. A large Union army from Kansas marched on Locust Grove. The Cherokee Confederate troops fought fiercely in defense of their home territory. However, they were outnumbered and suffered defeat. The Union soldiers then marched on Tahlequah, the capital. They captured Cherokee Chief John Ross and returned to Kansas.

During 1863 a Union army again invaded

northeastern Indian Territory. Union troops captured Fort Gibson and remained in Oklahoma. They used Fort Gibson as a base to improve their position in Indian Territory. General James Blunt was in command.

Confederate officials were concerned over Union army success in Indian Territory. They feared that Union armies from Fort Gibson might march into southern Arkansas. Northern Louisiana and Texas also were threatened. The officials ordered Cooper to drive the Union invaders back to Kansas.

During July, 1863, Cooper prepared his Confederate troops for an attack on Fort Gibson. Most of his men were at Fort Smith. Spies informed General Blunt of Cooper's plan. He marched his troops out to meet Cooper's army. On July 17 they met at Honey Springs in a battle that lasted all day. There were loud artillery exchanges, fierce cavalry charges, and hand-to-hand combat. Union troops defeated the Confederate Indian army.

After the victory at Honey Springs, Blunt marched his army south into the Choctaw nation and captured and burned Perryville, a Confederate supply depot. His Union army then moved east on Fort Smith and captured this post on September 1, 1863.

Civil War on the Plains—Most Oklahoma Indians were engaged in the Civil War in eastern Indian Territory. However some tribes were active in western Oklahoma, the Texas Panhandle, and eastern New Mexico. During 1862, Union troops drove Confederate armies out of New Mexico and Arizona. They controlled that territory until the close of the war. The Union base of operations was at Santa Fe in New Mexico.

Union armies on the Río Grande were supplied by wagon trains. Each month supply caravans moved over a military road which ran from Fort Leavenworth in Kansas to forts in New Mexico.

Comanche and Kiowa raiders from western Oklahoma preyed on these wagon trains. They captured food, blankets, and other supplies. General James Carleton was commander of Union troops in New Mexico. He ordered Colonel Kit Carson to take an army onto the plains and guard the wagon trains. Carson and his men rode over the plains of eastern New Mexico into the Texas Panhandle and on into western Oklahoma searching for Indian raiders.

115

71.   Artist's sketch depicting the Battle of Honey Springs.

72. General James G. Blunt, commander of Union troops in Indian Territory.

Several times troops from New Mexico met Comanches and Kiowas in combat. Their bloodiest battle occurred on November 25, 1864, at Adobe Walls, an old trading post situated on the Canadian River in the Texas Panhandle. Union scouts found a large Comanche-Kiowa village there. Carson struck the encampment with a surprise attack. After a day of fighting, the Union army withdrew, having failed to defeat the Indians.

Conclusion of the Civil War in Oklahoma—By 1863 the Union army controlled the northern half of Indian Territory. The Confederate Indian army held the territory south of the Arkansas and Canadian rivers. From that time until the close of the war there was only small-scale fighting in Oklahoma. Confederate Indian troops tried to drive the Union army out of Oklahoma.

Confederate officials promoted Colonel Stand Watie to brigadier general in 1864. They placed him in command of most of the Confederate troops in Oklahoma. Watie's base was south of the Canadian River. He sent his cavalry to raid Union positions in the Cherokee nation. Watie's swift strikes threatened Fort Gibson.

117

General Watie's greatest victory over Union troops in Oklahoma was at the Battle of Cabin Creek. It occurred during September, 1864. Watie's scouts discovered a large Union supply train of 300 wagons moving from Fort Scott in Kansas to Fort Gibson. The caravan was escorted by a heavy mounted guard. Watie's men attacked the wagon train at the Cabin Creek crossing in the Cherokee nation. The Confederate Cherokees defeated the Union army guarding the supply train. They drove the supply train into Confederate territory. Watie shared the captured food, clothing, medical supplies, and blankets with Confederate Indian refugees who lived in camps along Red River.

The Confederate Surrender—Watie's victories had little effect on the outcome of the war. Confederate armies in the eastern United States suffered smashing defeats by Union armies. General Ulysses S. Grant was commander of Union armies. General Robert E. Lee was commander of Confederate armies. On April 9, 1865, General Lee surrendered to General Grant at Appomattox Courthouse in Virginia. Confederate commanders in the West then began to surrender.

Confederate Indian officers in Oklahoma surrendered to Union officials at Doaksville in the Choctaw nation. Stand Watie was the last Confederate general to surrender. He offered his sword to Union officials at Doaksville on June 23, 1865.

RECONSTRUCTION IN OKLAHOMA

After the Confederate surrenders, the United States government set the method for Confederate states and territories to return to the Union. This method was called Reconstruction. It required each Confederate state or territory to free the slaves and to accept them as citizens. Reconstruction was applied to the governments of the Indian nations of Oklahoma.

The Fort Smith Council—Federal officials called leaders of the Five Civilized Tribes to meet with them at a council in Fort Smith. The Fort Smith Council began on September 8, 1865, and lasted thirteen days. Dennis Cooley, the commissioner of Indian Affairs, was in charge of the meeting.

Cooley told the Indian leaders that they had lost all treaty rights with the United States because they had joined the Confederacy.

118

Before each tribe could return to the Union, it had to sign a treaty of peace with the United States. The Indian nations had to abolish slavery and grant tribal citizenship to the freed blacks. Also, each Indian nation was required to surrender tribal land to the United States. Federal officials planned to settle other Indians on land taken from the Oklahoma Indians.

Tribal leaders opposed the terms of peace. Cooley was anxious to end the council but he saw that he would be unable to complete the Reconstruction Treaties at Fort Smith. The Indian leaders were too close to their homes and they were influenced by local public opinion. He ordered the tribal leaders to meet with him in Washington the following year, where they would be removed from the influence of their tribesmen. There the federal officials could manage them easier. But before the Fort Smith Council ended, Cooley signed a simple treaty of peace with each of the Five Civilized Tribes. It provided for an official end of the war.

The Little Arkansas Council—During the late summer of 1865, federal officials also called the leaders of the Comanches and Kiowas to a council. It was held at the mouth of the Little Arkansas River in south-central Kansas. Meeting with the Oklahoma tribes were the Cheyennes and Arapahoes. These two tribes roamed the territory north of the Arkansas River into eastern Colorado. Like the Comanches and Kiowas, they were buffalo hunters and fierce warriors.

The federal government planned to punish the Plains tribes for raiding Union supply lines during the Civil War. Tribal leaders were expected to sign the Little Arkansas Treaties, which assigned each tribe to a reservation. The Cheyenne and Arapaho tribes were assigned a reservation situated between the Arkansas River and the Cimarron River. It extended across western Kansas and Oklahoma. The Comanches and Kiowas were assigned a reservation situated between the Cimarron and Red rivers. It extended across western Oklahoma into the Texas Panhandle. The Plains tribes were expected to give up their wandering life and remain on these reservations.

The Reconstruction Treaties—The tribes of western Oklahoma and the Five Civilized Tribes were punished for helping the Confed-

119

73.   A Creek freedman's household.

74.   Cheyenne delegation to Washington.

eracy. The most severe punishment was loss of tribal land.

During 1856 leaders of the Five Civilized Tribes journeyed to Washington. They met with federal officials and signed the Reconstruction Treaties. The Choctaws and Chickasaws signed a joint treaty. Each treaty contained a clause abolishing slavery. The Creeks, Cherokees, Choctaws, Seminoles, and Chickasaws were required to grant tribal citizenship to the freed blacks. Also the tribes granted land to railway companies and permitted construction of rail lines across Oklahoma.

The Reconstruction Treaties revised the map of Indian Territory. The Creeks signed over to the federal government the western half of their nation. The Seminoles surrendered all of their land to the United States. They were assigned a small territory on the western border of the reduced Creek nation. The Choctaws and Chickasaws sold the Leased District to the United States. The Cherokees gave up a small tract in southeastern Kansas called the Neutral Lands. The federal government planned to settle other tribes in the Cherokee Outlet. By these Reconstruction Treaties the federal government took the western half of Oklahoma away from the Five Civilized Tribes.

The Civil War and Reconstruction had serious effects on the Indian tribes of Oklahoma. The Plains tribes were assigned to reservations. The Five Civilized Tribes lost much of their territory, and their governments were weakened. The year 1866 marked the beginning of the end for Indian Territory. Very soon the federal government would take other steps to weaken the tribal governments. By 1906 the Indians of Oklahoma had been forced into a new way of life.

CHAPTER SEVEN

Last Days of Indian Territory

The period from 1866 to 1889 was a busy time in Oklahoma. In eastern Indian Territory the Five Civilized Tribes were recovering from the Civil War. In western Indian Territory the federal government was forcing the buffalo-hunting tribes to settle on reservations. And federal officials were resettling tribes from other parts of the United States. They placed these Indians on land taken from the Five Civilized Tribes. This was a time of rapid change for the Indian people.

POSTWAR LIFE IN EASTERN INDIAN TERRITORY

The war had serious effects on the Five Civilized Tribes. Most of the men had served either the Confederate or the Union cause. Invading armies had scattered the civilian population. Thousands of Union Creeks, Seminoles, and Cherokees had fled to southern Kansas, where they lived in camps, waiting for the war to end. Confederate Indian refugees lived in camps along the Red River.

War had reduced the Five Civilized Tribes' population by at least one-fourth. Smallpox and cholera epidemics infected both Union and Confederate refugee camps. Hundred of Indian soldiers had died of battle wounds. The Cherokee, Creek, and Seminole nations were wastelands. Union and Confederate armies had burned and destroyed towns, churches, schools, and homes and had taken most of

123

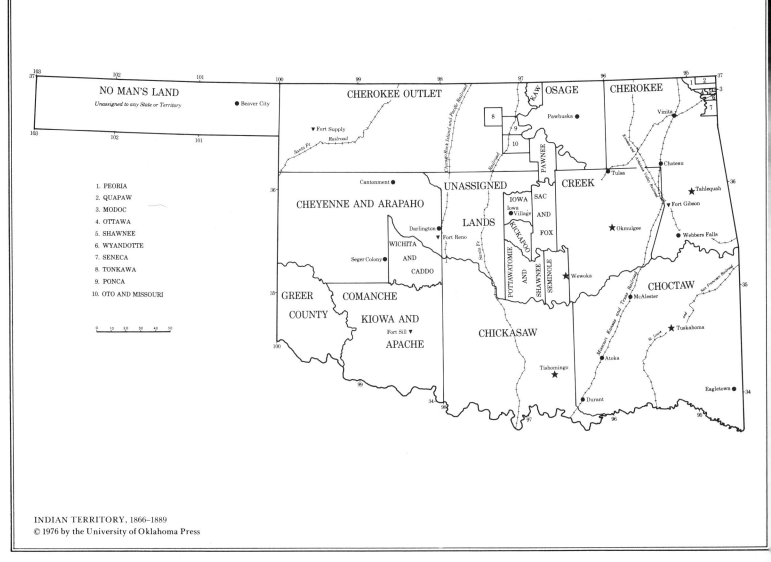

Indian Territory, 1866–1889

the livestock, grain, tools, and personal property. The Choctaw and Chickasaw nations had escaped the destruction of war. However, most of their livestock and food had been used to feed the Confederate army and refugees.

Restoring Tribal Governments—At first the tribal governments were unable to recover from the war. Tribal treasuries were empty. There were no funds to pay for law enforcement, schools, and other public services.

Lack of law enforcement attracted many criminals who used Indian Territory as a hideout. Outlaws robbed banks, stagecoaches, and trains, stole cattle and horses, and committed other crimes in the surrounding states. Then they rushed to their Indian Territory hideouts. Many famous Western criminals lived in Indian Territory after the Civil War. Among them were Belle Starr, the Younger brothers, the James brothers, and Ned Christie, the Cherokee bandit.

Leaders of the Five Civilized Tribes were unable to maintain law and order. They asked the national government for help and federal officials cooperated. They appointed a large

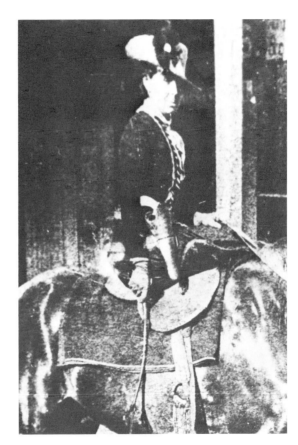

75. Belle Starr, famous outlaw of Indian Territory.

125

number of deputy United States marshals for Indian Territory. They established a federal district court at Fort Smith which was to try the criminals caught hiding in Indian Territory. Isaac Parker was the famous judge at this court. Deputy United States marshals patrolled Indian Territory. They arrested many outlaws and took them to the Fort Smith court for trial. Judge Parker became known as the "hanging judge of Fort Smith." Eighty-eight convicted outlaws were hung on the Fort Smith gallows.

Another postwar problem for the Indian governments was receiving the other tribes being sent to their lands. Most of the tribes were settled in the western half of Indian Territory. Their reservations were on land taken from the Five Civilized Tribes. But several tribes were settled in eastern Oklahoma. In the northeastern corner of Indian Territory lived Quapaws, Senecas, and Shawnees. Federal officials took a portion of the land belonging to these tribes and relocated several tribes from Kansas, including the Wyandots, Peorias, Miamis, and Ottawas. These Indians began arriving in Oklahoma in 1867.

During 1873 the federal government moved the Modocs, a California tribe, to northeastern Indian Territory. The Modocs had fought settlers invading their territory until the United States Army had defeated them. Nearly 200 of the Modocs who surrendered were brought to Indian Territory.

The federal government moved several tribes into the Cherokee nation. In 1867, 1,000 Delawares moved from northern Kansas. They settled in the Verdigris valley of the Cherokee nation. Cherokees adopted the Delawares as tribal citizens. In 1867 about 700 Shawnees moved from Kansas to the Cherokee nation. The Shawnees settled in present Craig County. They, also, were adopted as citizens of the Cherokee nation.

The freedmen, former slaves, were another problem for the governments of the Five Civilized Tribes. The Indian nations had to accept their former slaves as citizens and give them land. After the Civil War the southern states segregated the former slaves. By segregation is meant that the blacks had to live in certain parts of the towns and black children had to attend separate schools. The Five Civilized Tribes copied this system. Tribal governments adopted laws which segregated the

76. Black homesteader family and dugout dwelling in the Unassigned Lands of Oklahoma.

former slaves. Blacks had to live in settlements apart from the Indian towns. This explains why we have Boley, Foreman, Red Bird, Rentiesville, and other all-black towns in Oklahoma today. The tribal governments also adopted laws segregating black children in schools.

Prosperity returned to Oklahoma about 1869. Farming, ranching, mining, and railroad building helped the Indian nations. Prosperity brought funds to the tribal treasuries. Tribal officials could open schools and courts and resume law enforcement.

Economic Recovery—Soon after the close of the war, Indian leaders rebuilt old towns and founded new towns. They expanded Oklahoma's transportation system. New stage and mail lines, freighting companies and river steamboat companies were founded. Indian farmers cleared undergrowth from old fields and opened new fields. Ranchmen restocked their ranges. Soon grain, hides, lead, and salt cargoes moved on flatboats and steamers to market. Herds of horses and cattle from Indian Territory ranches were sold in the markets of Arkansas and Missouri.

Building the railroads helped Oklahoma's

recovery from the ruin of war. In 1870 the Missouri, Kansas and Texas Railway Company, called the Katy, began construction in Indian Territory. By the close of 1871 the railroad crossed Red River into Texas. Freight and passenger trains moved across eastern Oklahoma. In 1870 the Frisco Railroad entered Oklahoma from Seneca, Missouri. It was built to Vinita. Soon it would extend to Tulsa and points west. The Fort Smith and Western, the Choctaw and Gulf, the Santa Fe, and the Rock Island railroads also crossed Oklahoma. Many new towns grew up along the railroad lines.

Ranching was an important industry in Oklahoma after the war. Indians of the Five Civilized Tribes began to raise livestock soon after they reached Indian Territory. They established fine herds of cattle and horses, but most of their livestock was destroyed by the war. After 1866, Indian Territory ranchers rebuilt their herds.

Before railroads came, Indian Territory was a great cattle highway for Texas cattle. Texas ranges were crowded with cattle, while in the eastern United States beef prices were high. Railroad companies had extended lines

77. Farmer breaking land for cotton.

78. Plains farmer using sod-plow, the cutting tool used to open Oklahoma's western grasslands to agriculture.

79. Railroad building in Indian Territory.

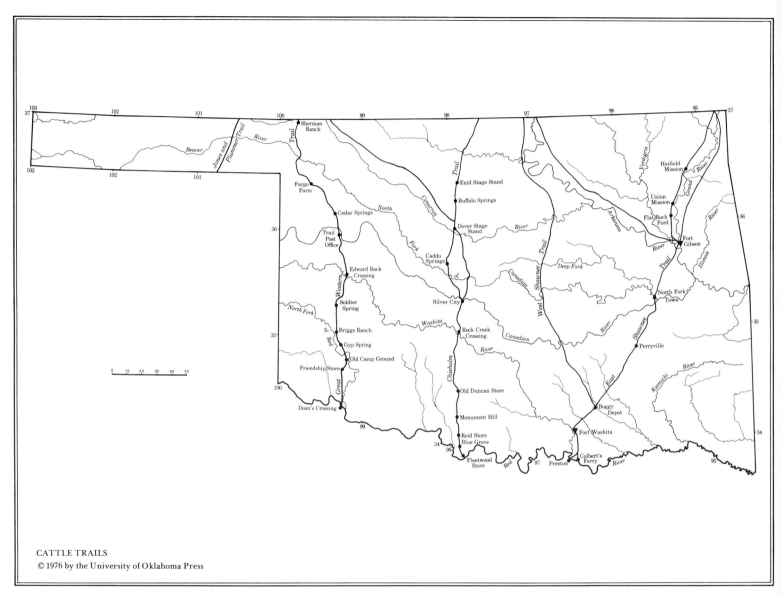

Cattle Trails Through Oklahoma

80.   Texas trail herd crossing Indian Territory, 1888.

81.   Cowboys resting while the cattle drink at a lake on the plains about 1890.

across Missouri and were building in eastern Kansas. In 1866, Texas cattlemen began to drive their herds to the railroad towns in Kansas. There the cattle were loaded in stock cars and carried to eastern markets.

The cattle trails to the Kansas cow towns crossed Oklahoma. The first cattle trail was the East Shawnee Trail. It crossed Red River at Colbert's Ferry, following the Texas Road to Baxter Springs, Kansas. The West Shawnee Trail branched toward Abilene at Boggy Depot. Abilene was the most important Kansas cow town. The Chisholm Trail was the greatest cattle highway in the West. It crossed central Indian Territory. Most of the Texas cattle marketed in the Kansas cow towns moved up the Chisholm Trail. The fourth cattle highway which crossed Indian Territory was the Dodge City or Great Western Cattle Trail. It crossed Red River at Doan's Store into the Leased District and on to Dodge City. After rail lines were built across Indian Territory, ranchmen used railroads to ship their cattle to market.

After the Civil War, mining was another important industry. Lead mining was carried on in northeastern Oklahoma. However, the most important mineral industry in this period was coal mining. Most of the early-day coal mining was in the Choctaw nation near McAlester. Some coal was also mined in the Creek and Cherokee nations. Railroad companies operated the mines. Coal from Indian Territory mines was ideal for firing the locomotives' steam boilers.

Skilled miners were scarce in Indian Territory. Mining companies imported thousands of miners from the eastern United States and from Europe. Miners and their families came to Oklahoma from Italy, Greece, Germany, Russia, Poland, and England. Coal-mining companies paid the Indian governments a royalty of ten cents for each ton of coal mined from their lands. The income from coal mining helped the Indian governments to recover from the Civil War.

The rapid economic development in eastern Indian Territory required many workers. Thousands of workers from the surrounding states came to take jobs in Indian Territory, and most immigrants brought their families. Soon they were more numerous than Indians and freedmen.

But the only persons who had a right to

135

82.   Permit holder and family, Chickasaw nation, 1896.

83. Early-day farm family in the Chickasaw nation.

live in Indian Territory were citizens of the Indian nations. These included former slaves who were now freedmen. To control the thousands of white and black workers flooding into Oklahoma, the Indian governments adopted the permit system. Each worker entering the Cherokee, Creek, Choctaw, Seminole, or Chickasaw nation had to buy a permit from the tribal government. The cost of the permit was five dollars a year. By 1900 there were more permit holders in Indian Territory than Indians. The intruders began to demand political rights. Their demands led to the end of Indian governments.

POSTWAR LIFE
IN WESTERN INDIAN TERRITORY

In western Oklahoma conditions were quite different from those in eastern Oklahoma after the Civil War. The federal government had taken the western half of Indian Territory from the Five Civilized Tribes. Federal officials planned to carve this area into reservations. Here they intended to settle tribes from other parts of the United States. Most of the tribes settled peacefully on their new reservations, but a few of them resisted. The United States Army waged a long and bloody war against these tribes. Finally they surrendered and moved to their reservations in western Oklahoma.

The Peaceful Relocations—One of the first tribes to move to Oklahoma after the Civil War was the Osage. This tribe, which numbered over 1,500, gave up the reservation in southern Kansas. By 1872 they had settled on their Indian Territory reservation, situated between the 96th meridian and the Arkansas River in the eastern portion of the Cherokee Outlet.

The Kaws, who were closely related to the Osages in language and culture and who numbered about 500, exchanged their Kansas reservation for a 100,000-acre tract in the northwest corner of the Osage reservation. The Kaws settled on their Oklahoma reservation home in 1873. The Osage and Kaw tribes were under the authority of the Osage Agency at Pawhuska.

The Sac and Fox tribes resided in Kansas and Iowa. During 1867 the federal government assigned these Indians a reservation in central Indian Territory. By 1869 the Sac and

84. Sac and Fox Indians and whites at a trading post on the Sac and Fox Reservation, Indian Territory, about 1889.

Fox tribes had moved to the new reservation in Oklahoma.

Next to the Sac and Fox reservation on the west, federal officials settled 450 Potawatomis from Kansas. A band of Shawnees and 250 Iowas from the Kansas and Nebraska area settled on the same reservation. Next to the Shawnees in central Oklahoma, federal agents settled a band of 350 Mexican Kickapoos. They had been living on a reservation in the north Mexican state of Coahuila. In 1873 the federal government forced many of the Mexican Kickapoos to return to the United States. They settled on the Oklahoma reservation. The tribes in central Oklahoma were under the Sac and Fox Agency near Stroud.

85. Potawatomi girls of the Indian Territory
    in the 1880's, photographed by
    W. S. Prettyman. As shown in *A History
    of the Indians of the United States,*
    by Angie Debo.

Federal agents relocated 680 Poncas from Dakota Territory. In 1876 the Poncas settled on a reservation near the Chikaskia River in the Cherokee Outlet. South of the Poncas, federal officials created a small reservation. On it they settled 400 Otos and Missouris. These Indians had been living on a reservation on the Kansas-Nebraska border. The Otos and Missouris reached the Indian Territory between 1880 and 1883. The Pawnees, who lived on a reservation in Nebraska, numbered about 2,000. Federal agents assigned them a reservation in the Cherokee Outlet.

The Nez Percés lived in Idaho and eastern Washington. Under their great war leader Chief Joseph, the Nez Percés fought a long war against the United States Army. Finally Chief Joseph surrendered in 1877. Federal officials moved the Nez Percés, numbering about 450, to Indian Territory. They settled in the Cherokee Outlet on a reservation near the Chikaskia River. Nez Percés leaders begged the federal government to return them to their northern homeland. Finally, in 1885, they were permitted to return.

The Tonkawas were a Texas tribe who had been living in the Leased District since 1859. They numbered about one hundred. In 1885 they were relocated in the Cherokee Outlet. The Poncas, Pawnees, Otos, Missouris, for a time the Nez Percés, and the Tonkawas were under the Ponca Agency.

Federal officials set aside a reservation on the Washita River for Indians who had lived in the Leased District before the Civil War. These Indians consisted of 1,100 Wichitas, Caddoes, and Delawares. Also included were the Texas tribes. They had been colonized in the Leased District before the Civil War. The Texas tribes included the Keechis, Anadarkos, Ionis, and Wacos. They were under the Wichita Agency situated near present Anadarko.

Government agents tried to direct the lives of Indians on these Oklahoma reservations. The aim of the federal government was to erase their native customs. Agents tried to lead the Indians along the road to white civilization. Federal officials established schools on the reservations to educate Indian children. Adult Indians were expected to take up farming. Most of the Indian tribes accepted reservation homes in Oklahoma and remained at peace with the United States. However, the Indians were proud of their native heri-

141

86.   Hide hunters camped on the Southern Plains.

87.   Comanche village scene near Fort Sill, 1879.

tage and most of them refused to give up their Indian ways.

Conquest of the Plains Tribes—The buffalo-hunting tribes were not so easy to deal with. They had great military power. Federal officials planned to settle them on small reservations in western Oklahoma. In 1865, leaders of these tribes had signed the Little Arkansas Treaties, which reduced their hunting territories. However, they still had large reservations on which to hunt buffalo. Soon federal officials saw that the reservations would have to be reduced because pioneers were settling on these lands. White hunters were slaughtering the buffalo, and these tribes depended upon the buffalo for food, shelter, and clothing. Satanta of the Kiowas and Ten Bears of the Comanches threatened to make war on the pioneers.

To keep the peace, federal officials called the leaders of the Plains tribes to another council. During October, 1867, federal agents and tribal leaders met on Medicine Lodge Creek in southwestern Kansas. At the council they negotiated new agreements. By the Medicine Lodge Treaties, the Cheyennes and Arapahoes were assigned a much smaller reservation in west-central Indian Territory. The Comanches and Kiowas were assigned a much smaller reservation in southwestern Indian Territory.

Federal officials believed that they would have to use military force to keep the Plains tribes on their small reservations. Soldiers of the United States Army established several forts on the reservations. Fort Supply was constructed in 1868 on the upper edge of the Cheyenne-Arapaho reservation. Fort Sill was erected in 1869 in the Wichita Mountains, in the heart of the Comanche-Kiowa reservation. In 1874, Fort Reno was established in the center of the Cheyenne-Arapaho reservation. The Cheyennes and Arapahoes were under the Darlington Agency near Fort Reno. The Comanche and Kiowa agency was near Fort Sill.

Comanches, Kiowas, Cheyennes, and Arapahoes left their reservations to hunt buffalo and to raid settlements. Federal officials were determined to force them to accept reservation life. Between 1868 and 1874 there were many battles in western Oklahoma between Indians and soldiers.

88. Indian police, Fort Reno, 1887.

89. Black Kettle, Cheyenne chief slain at the Battle of the Washita.

In late November, 1868, Colonel George Custer led the Seventh Cavalry out of Fort Supply. He was searching for Indians. At daybreak on November 27, Custer and his troops reached the Washita River. Scouts found an Indian village, a Cheyenne camp led by Black Kettle. Custer ordered a surprise attack and the Seventh Cavalry killed more than one hundred warriors. They took fifty women and children prisoners. Chief Black Kettle was among those slain. The soldiers burned the village and captured a large herd of horses. The Battle of the Washita was the first of many campaigns against the Plains tribes.

Troops from Fort Supply, Fort Sill, and Fort Reno patrolled the reservations. They watched the movements of the Indians. Warriors slipped away from their reservations on foot, raided ranches and farms in Texas and Kansas for horses and guns, then attacked the settlements. By 1874 their raids had become so widespread that the War Department decided to conquer the Plains tribes.

General Nelson Miles was placed in command of a large army. His troops moved across western Oklahoma and the Texas Panhandle. They defeated many warrior bands. Other

bands came in to the reservations and surrendered.

Cheyenne and Arapaho bands surrendered at Darlington Agency. Kiowa and Comanche bands surrendered at Fort Sill. The last warriors to surrender were the Quahada Comanches led by Quanah Parker. Parker surrendered on June 24, 1875. Troops at Fort Sill, Fort Reno, and Fort Supply seized the warriors' horses and weapons and arrested the Indian leaders. Soldiers placed seventy-two chiefs under heavy guard and took them to military prison at Fort Marion, in St. Augustine, Florida.

One band of Indians from Arizona was settled on the Comanche-Kiowa reservation. Geronimo and his Apache followers had made war on the settlements of the Southwest. He surrendered to army officers in 1886. Federal officials sent Geronimo and 400 followers— men, women, and children—to military pris-

90.   Comanche war chief Quanah Parker.

on in Florida. During 1888 the Apache prisoners were moved to Mount Vernon Barracks in Alabama. There many Apaches died from tuberculosis. In 1894 the Apaches were settled on the Comanche-Kiowa reservation.

Peace had come to the Indian Territory. The Plains tribes had been conquered. With sadness the Plains tribes settled down to dull lives on the reservations. They had hardly taken up the new life when the federal government took their reservations and opened the land to settlers. Thus Oklahoma Territory was born.

91. Comanche girls, settled in Indian Territory after the wars with the Plains Indians. On the right is Mary Parker, daughter of Quanah Parker.

CHAPTER EIGHT

Oklahoma Territory

By 1880 most of the good land in the West had been settled. Many Americans had not received a free homestead of 160 acres of government land. Indian Territory had much fine farming land but it was closed to homesteading because the land in Oklahoma belonged to the Indian tribes. Treaties with the United States government protected their title to the land. The Indians seemed to be safe from settlers. But already men were working to open the reservation lands so that settlers could homestead in Oklahoma.

REMOVING THE OBSTACLES TO SETTLEMENT

Congress had the power to change treaties with the Indian tribes. Treaties guaranteed Indian ownership of the reservation lands. Many congressmen believed that too much land already had been taken from the Indians. Their land in Oklahoma should be preserved. Yet other powerful men urged Congress to adopt laws to permit settlement in Oklahoma. Then settlers could take homesteads there.

The Boomers — The railroad companies worked to open Oklahoma to settlement. The Katy, Frisco, Rock Island, and Santa Fe lines crossed Indian Territory. Railway companies wanted Oklahoma more thickly settled because more freight and passengers would mean more profits for the rail lines. Thus

92.   Railroad building in the Cherokee Outlet, 1899.

railroad companies urged Congress to open Indian Territory for homesteading.

A group of promoters called Boomers also worked to open Indian Territory to settlement. They promoted Oklahoma across the United States. Boomers described Oklahoma's rich land and resources before large audiences in the East. They wrote newspaper articles describing Oklahoma as a Garden of Eden.

The leading Boomers were Charles C. Carpenter, Elias C. Boudinot, David L. Payne, and William L. Couch. They led settlers to the border of Indian Territory and established Boomer camps in southern Kansas and northern Texas. The people in these camps waited for Oklahoma to be opened to settlement. Then they could rush in and take a homestead farm of 160 acres.

David L. Payne led Boomer raids. Homeseekers from the Boomer camps entered Oklahoma and settled on an attractive spot. Troops from forts in Indian Territory arrested the leaders of the Boomer raids and forced the settlers to return to Kansas and Texas. Boomer raids popularized Indian Territory across the nation. They called attention to

93.   David L. Payne, leader of the Boomers.

151

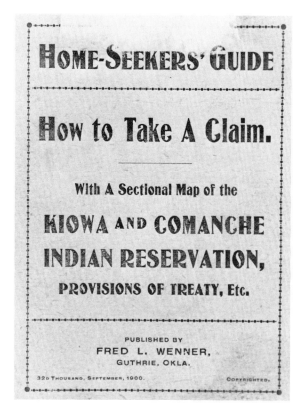

HOME-SEEKERS' GUIDE

How to Take A Claim.

With A Sectional Map of the

KIOWA AND COMANCHE
INDIAN RESERVATION,

PROVISIONS OF TREATY, Etc.

PUBLISHED BY
FRED L. WENNER,
GUTHRIE, OKLA.

32b THOUSAND, SEPTEMBER, 1900.   COPYRIGHTED.

94.   Boomer literature.

this area and encouraged settlement. They pressed Congress to remove tribal title to the lands so that homesteaders could enter Oklahoma legally. Boomer raids and publicity began to have an effect on Congress.

Allotment in Severalty—Before Indian Territory could be opened to homesteaders, tribal title to the land had to be removed. The Indian tribes held their lands in common which means that ownership of the land was vested in the tribe. During the 1880's leaders in Congress decided that the reservation system was a failure. They wished to change Indian culture. Congressmen believed the way to do this was to destroy tribal governments and tribal ownership of land. They decided to break up the reservations. Each Indian would receive an allotment of 160 acres of land. Government leaders believed that making an Indian a landowner would change his culture.

Changing from tribal ownership to individual ownership is called allotment in severalty. In 1887, Congress passed the Dawes Allotment Act. It provided for dividing the Indian reservations of Oklahoma into 160-acre tracts. Government agents were to assign each In-

95. Indians awaiting land allotments at Union Agency, Muskogee, 1899.

96.   Enrollment-Allotment headquarters, Cherokee nation.

dian a 160-acre homestead. This was called an allotment. Any land remaining was declared surplus. The surplus land was to be opened to settlement by homesteaders. At this time the Dawes Act did not apply to the Five Civilized Tribes.

A federal commission called the Jerome Commission was appointed to direct the

change from tribal to individual ownership. The Jerome Commission was to assign allotments of land to Indians. Members of the Jerome Commission traveled to Indian Territory and met with tribal leaders. By 1901, the Jerome Commission had completed allotment agreements with all the tribes of western Oklahoma. The Jerome Commission assigned

154

each Indian an allotment of 160 acres. Millions of acres remained, which the federal government declared to be surplus land. Officials prepared to open it to settlement by homesteaders.

HOMESTEADING IN OKLAHOMA TERRITORY

Congress had removed the obstacles to settlement in Indian Territory. By 1906 all of Oklahoma west of the territory of the Five Civilized Tribes had been opened to settlement. The Indian reservations had been changed to counties in the new Territory of Oklahoma. Homesteaders received farms in Oklahoma Territory by land runs and a lottery. The arrival of homesteaders in Oklahoma brought the pioneer period to Indian Territory.

The Land Runs—The first portion of Indian Territory opened to settlement was the Unassigned Lands. This was a 2,000,000-acre tract in the center of Indian Territory. Federal officials surveyed the area and laid out townsites. Only about 10,000 claims of 160 acres each remained. They expected more homeseekers than homesteads were available, so in order to give all homeseekers an equal chance, they decided to open the Unassigned Lands by a land run.

Several days before the opening, settlers began gathering on the borders of the Unassigned Lands. They camped and waited. April 22, 1889, was the day set for the opening. Over 50,000 homeseekers were ready. At noon on that day, soldiers guarding the borders of the Unassigned Lands used pistols and bugles to give the signal. The race for homesteads began. Homeseekers rushed into the Unassigned Lands on horseback, in wagons, on bicycles, and on trains. There were even some on foot. By evening of April 22 every homestead had been staked, and homeseekers had staked town lots in Guthrie, Kingfisher, Oklahoma City, and Norman.

Nearly one thousand blacks made the run of 1889. Most of them were from the South. Many blacks obtained homesteads. Most of them settled east of Guthrie. Langston was an all-black town established by these pioneers.

In 1891 another portion of Indian Territory was opened to homesteaders by a land run. The Jerome Commission had completed

155

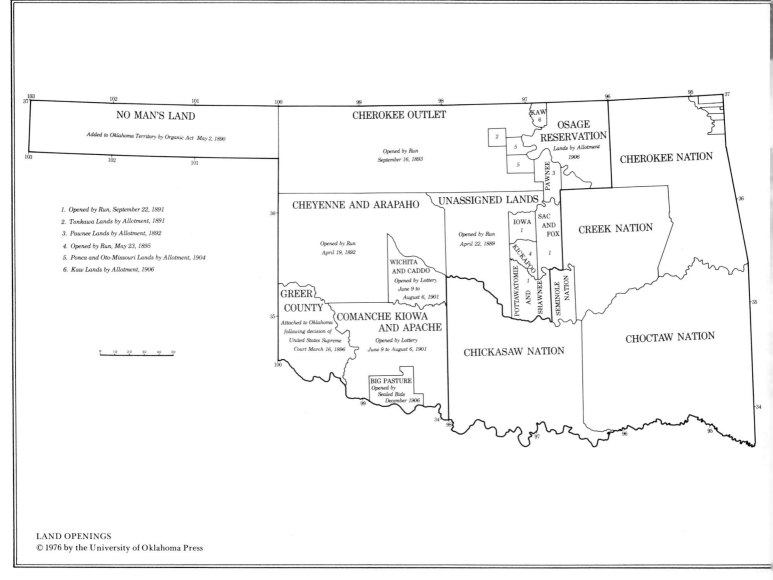

Land Openings in Oklahoma

97.   Artist's sketch of Land Run of 1889 for a homestead in the Unassigned Lands.

98.   Recorder's tent and office, Guthrie, Oklahoma, 1889.

99.   Future site of Oklahoma City on the morning of April 22, 1889. By late afternoon, the space around the depot was covered by tents.

100.   Oklahoma City street scene soon after the land run of 1889.

101.   Preparation for the opening of the Cherokee Outlet, 1893.

102.   Land run scene. Cherokee Outlet, 1893.

an allotment agreement with the Sac, Fox, Potawatomi, Shawnee, and Iowa tribes. Federal officials opened their surplus lands to settlement on September 22, 1891. Over 20,000 persons raced for homesteads in the central Indian Territory reservations.

The next year federal officials opened another reservation. On April 19, 1892, homesteaders settled the surplus lands of the Cheyennes and Arapahoes by a land run. About 25,000 persons raced for homesteads in Cheyenne-Arapaho country.

During 1893 the Cherokee Outlet was opened. This was the largest land run in history. More than 100,000 settlers raced for homesteads in the Cherokee Outlet. The final land run in Indian Territory occurred in 1895. In that year the Kickapoo reservation was opened to settlement.

For the next land opening in Indian Territory, federal officials used the lottery. During August, 1901, the surplus lands of the Kiowa, Comanche, Apache, Wichita, and Caddo reservations were opened to settlement. About 165,000 homeseekers registered at Fort Sill and Fort Reno. Officials then held a drawing to distribute the 15,000 homesteads.

Federal officials withdrew several large tracts in the Kiowa-Comanche country from settlement. These lands were the Fort Sill Military Reservation of 56,000 acres, the Wichita Mountain Forest Reserve of 58,000 acres, and the Big Pasture Reserve of 480,000 acres. The Big Pasture was a grazing tract reserved for the Kiowas and Comanches. In 1906 federal officials sold the Big Pasture at public auction.

Several small reservations in north-central Indian Territory were allotted before 1906. Federal officials allotted the Ponca, Oto, Missouri, and Kaw reservations in 1904. After the Oto and Missouri reservation was allotted, 51,000 acres remained as surplus. Federal officials sold this land to settlers. The Osage reservation was allotted in 1906. There was no surplus land for settlers on the Osage reservation.

After each reservation was allotted and settled, it was shifted from Indian Territory to Oklahoma Territory. During the territorial period, bits and pieces of land were added to complete the western half of Oklahoma. A federal law passed in 1890 attached the Panhandle to Oklahoma Territory. There was a large tract of territory in question south of

163

El Reno streets time of Drawing 1901

103.   Lottery drawing at El Reno for homesteads in the Kiowa-Comanche country, 1901.

104. Waiting to register for a claim in the great land lottery, Fort Reno, 1901.

105. Frontier lawyer's office, Anadarko, Oklahoma Territory, following the great land lottery, 1901.

106.   Store in Anadarko, Oklahoma Territory, after the 1901 land lottery.

the North Fork of Red River. Texas claimed this land and had organized it into Greer County. In 1896 the United States Supreme Court denied Texas' claim and awarded Greer County to Oklahoma Territory. By allotment, land runs, a lottery, an auction, a law of Congress, and a Supreme Court decision, the western half of Oklahoma grew. In 1906 western Oklahoma had reached its present area and shape.

Oklahoma Pioneers—Most of the Oklahoma settlers were poor. They suffered great hardship until they adjusted to the Oklahoma environment. Money was scarce. The Oklahoma pioneer bartered for necessities. He traded eggs and butter for salt, sugar, and coffee. A homesteader might swap a horse or a cow for a year's supply of flour. For cash he gathered buffalo bones scattered across the plains and sold them to fertilizer companies for seven dollars a ton. The pioneer also cut cedar posts for building fences and sold them to ranchers for two cents each. Many settlers worked in the Kansas wheat harvest. They earned money to buy seed, plows, and livestock.

Providing shelter for his family was a prob-

lem for the Oklahoma pioneer. After staking his claim, the homesteader used a tent or canvas-covered wagon box for shelter. If there was timber on his homestead, he cut logs and built a cabin home. Most of central and western Oklahoma Territory was covered with grass. Where no timber was at hand, the settler used a dugout or a sod house. Most early dwellings in Oklahoma Territory were sod houses. The walls of the sod house were constructed of sod blocks. The blocks were cut from the deep-rooted grass on the homestead. The pioneer used a special cutting tool called the sod plow to slice through the thick sod. Pioneers also constructed school buildings and churches from logs or sod blocks.

The lack of timber in Oklahoma Territory made fuel for cooking and heating scarce. Many early-day settlers used "cow chips," dried buffalo or cattle dung, for fuel. Pioneer Oklahomans had to be self-reliant to survive.

Clearing thick, deep-rooted grass from fields required much time and hard work. Pioneer farmers rushed to prepare their fields for planting wheat, corn, cotton, and other cash crops. Gardens and orchards produced vegetables and fruits. Game was abundant, and

107.   Dugout residence of homesteader family near Guthrie, 1890.

108.   Sod house of homesteaders in western Oklahoma Territory.

109.   Homestead in the Cherokee Outlet, 1894. Note sod house behind the frame building.

Copyrighted 1909 by J. V. Dedrick

No 34.

Oklahoma Dugout.

110.   Oklahoma dugout.

111. Collecting "cow chips" for fuel.

the pioneer had to be a hunter. Wild turkey, prairie chicken, quail, deer, and rabbit were a regular part of the pioneer diet.

Early Oklahoma Towns—During the pioneer period, most Oklahomans lived in the country on homesteads. However, several towns grew up. The spread of railroads across Oklahoma Territory linked the new towns with markets across the nation. The Santa Fe, Rock Island, Choctaw and Gulf, and Frisco were the leading railroads in Oklahoma Territory.

Guthrie, Oklahoma City, Norman, Enid, Woodward, El Reno, Lawton, and other towns were situated on the railroad lines. They became regional trade centers. Pioneer farmers marketed grain, cotton, and livestock in these towns. Banking, farm and ranch supply, and other businesses developed. Guthrie was the territorial capital. Its population about 1890 was 6,000. At that time it was the largest town in Oklahoma Territory.

RISE OF OKLAHOMA GOVERNMENT

Oklahoma's present state government had its beginnings during the territorial period. Congress directed the creation of new states. A

173

112.   Norman, Oklahoma Territory, 1889.

113.   General store, Enid, Oklahoma Territory in old Cherokee Outlet, 1896.

114. El Reno, Oklahoma Territory, livery stable, showing horse-drawn hearse and buggies for hire.

frontier area was expected to pass through a training period, the territorial stage. The people in the new land learned to work together and gained experience in self-government. After some years in this training period of territorial government, Congress examined the territory to determine whether or not it was ready for statehood. Then Congress admitted the territory to the Union and it became a state. Oklahoma's territorial stage, its training period for statehood, extended from 1889 to 1907.

Oklahoma Territorial Government—Oklahoma pioneers came from all sections of the nation and from several foreign countries. They brought with them their religion, social customs, and political ideas. Soon after settlers reached Oklahoma, they formed political parties. These included the Republican party, Democratic party, Populist party, and Socialist party. The strongest parties in Oklahoma Territory were the Republican and Democratic parties.

The guide for forming a government for Oklahoma Territory was a law passed by Congress in 1890. It was the Oklahoma Organic Act. This law provided for a governor, a secretary, and a supreme court of three judges. These officials were appointed by the president of the United States. The Oklahoma Organic Act provided for a legislature and a congressional delegate. The voters of Oklahoma Territory elected the members of the legislature and the congressional delegate.

The Organic Act divided Oklahoma Territory into temporary counties. It provided for county and town government. The Organic Act required that the territorial capital be located at Guthrie.

Oklahoma territorial government began during 1890. President Benjamin Harrison appointed George W. Steele of Indiana to be governor. Through the years presidents appointed other men to the office of governor of Oklahoma Territory. They were Robert Martin (1891–92), Abraham J. Seay (1892–93), William C. Renfrow (1893–97), Cassius M. Barnes (1897–1901), and Frank Frantz (1906–1907). All of these men were Republicans except Governor Renfrow. He was a Democrat, appointed by Democratic President Grover Cleveland.

The congressional delegate was an impor-

177

tant official in the territorial government. He represented Oklahoma Territory in the Congress. It was his duty to protect and promote the interests of the people of the territory. He was to work for statehood for Oklahoma.

Congressional delegates elected from Oklahoma Territory were David Harvey (1890–93), Dennis Flynn (1893–97), James Y. Callahan (1897–99), Dennis Flynn (1899–1903), and Bird S. McGuire (1903–1907). All congressional delegates elected by the voters of Oklahoma Territory were Republican except James Y. Callahan. He was elected in 1896 by the combined Populist and Democratic parties of the territory.

During the territorial period, the Oklahoma legislature established the foundations of future state government. Laws adopted by the territorial legislature created the machinery of Oklahoma government. These laws organized counties and created courts. The territorial legislature established the system of public schools and began formation of the Oklahoma university and college system.

The first territorial legislature created three institutions of higher learning. These were the University of Oklahoma at Norman, the

115. Dennis Flynn, Territorial delegate to Congress.

116.   Woodward, Oklahoma Territory, 1894.

117. Guthrie, Oklahoma Territory, 1890.

118.   Tulsa, Indian Territory, 1890.

Oklahoma Agricultural and Mechanical College at Stillwater, and the Oklahoma Normal School at Edmond. The normal school was to train teachers for the public schools of Oklahoma Territory.

Oklahoma Statehood Movement—The chief concern of the people of Oklahoma Territory was statehood in the American Union. Each year they held statehood conventions. These conventions adopted resolutions urging Congress to grant statehood. However, Congress held up action on Oklahoma statehood because most congressmen believed that Oklahoma Territory should be joined with Indian Territory to form a single, larger state. Until this was done, Congress refused to take any final action on Oklahoma statehood.

PREPARING INDIAN TERRITORY FOR STATEHOOD

Before Oklahoma Territory and Indian Territory could be joined, the land system in Indian Territory had to be changed. The Five Civilized Tribes held their lands in common. Congressmen wished to abolish this system. In addition, Indian Territory was divided into five self-governing nations. Congress re-

quired that the tribal governments be abolished. After the land system was changed and the tribal governments abolished, Congress planned to join Indian Territory and Oklahoma Territory. Then it would admit the Twin Territories to the Union as the single state of Oklahoma.

Changing the Land System—In 1887, Congress had passed the Dawes Allotment Act, which provided for the end of tribal ownership of Indian lands. Each Indian was required to accept an allotment of land. This law had not applied to the Five Civilized Tribes. However, in 1893, Congress passed a law which extended the Dawes Allotment Act to the Five Civilized Tribes.

The President appointed the Dawes Commission to change the land system in Indian Territory. Senator Henry L. Dawes of Massachusetts was chairman of the Dawes Commission. The Commission traveled to Indian Territory, and the members spent several years trying to change the land system of the Five Civilized Tribes. Indian citizens preferred tribal ownership of lands and opposed accepting allotments. They had great respect for tradition, and the traditional system of land holding among Indians was common owner-ship.

Congress increased the powers of the Dawes Commission, so that it could assign allotments to Indians without approval of Indian leaders. This change caused the leaders of the Five Civilized Tribes finally to sign allotment agreements. The chiefs of the Choctaws and Chickasaws were the first to agree to allotment in severalty. Leaders of the other tribes followed, and by 1902 the Dawes Commission had signed allotment agreements with all of the Five Civilized Tribes.

The Dawes Commission then began to assign allotments to Indians and freedmen. There were no surplus lands for homesteading. Every acre of land in the eastern half of Oklahoma was allotted to tribal citizens.

Ending the Indian Governments—The governments of the Five Civilized Tribes were another obstacle to Oklahoma statehood. Congress believed that it had to erase the tribal governments. The Curtis Act, passed by Congress in 1898, ended tribal rule. It brought many changes in Indian Territory. The Curtis Act substituted federal laws for the laws of the Indian governments. It provided for the survey of townsites and it extended voting rights to over half a million non-Indians—the permit holders. The Curtis Act established a system of free public schools for the non-Indian children of Indian Territory. It abolished tribal courts and made Indian citizens subject to federal courts.

The Sequoyah Statehood Movement—Indian Territory was now ready for statehood. The Dawes Commission had changed the land system from tribal to individual ownership. The Curtis Act had erased the tribal governments. Congress was ready to join Indian Territory to Oklahoma Territory and form the single state of Oklahoma.

Leaders of the Five Civilized Tribes opposed joining Oklahoma Territory. They wanted to form an all-Indian state separate from Oklahoma in Indian Territory. They planned to call the all-Indian state Sequoyah. Leaders of the Five Civilized Tribes met at Muskogee in 1905. Creek Chief Pleasant Porter was elected president of the Sequoyah Convention. Alexander Posey, the Creek poet, was elected secretary. The delegates wrote a constitution for the proposed state of Sequoyah which was

183

119. Pleasant Porter. From *A History of the Indians of the United States,* by Angie Debo.

184

approved by the voters of Indian Territory. Tribal leaders sent the Sequoyah Constitution to Congress but congressmen refused to consider it. They were preparing to join the Twin Territories into the state of Oklahoma.

OKLAHOMA STATEHOOD

On June 16, 1906, Congress passed the Oklahoma Enabling Act. It permitted the people of Oklahoma Territory and Indian Territory to join together and write a constitution. The constitutional convention was to meet at Guthrie. It was to consist of 112 delegates. Fifty-five delegates were to be elected from Oklahoma Territory and fifty-five delegates were to be elected from Indian Territory. Two delegates were to be elected from the Osage nation.

The Oklahoma Constitutional Convention— During the summer of 1906 voters in the Twin Territories elected constitutional convention delegates. The Democratic delegates won one hundred of the convention seats, while Republicans won twelve seats. Thus Democrats were the convention leaders. The convention met at Guthrie in November, 1906. Democrat William H. Murray was elected president of

120. William H. Murray as president of the Oklahoma constitutional convention.

the convention. His majority floor leader was Charles N. Haskell. The Republican leader in the convention was Henry Asp.

The convention delegates worked through the winter and drafted a constitution which created three departments for the new government. The executive branch consisted of a governor and eleven other executive officials. The legislative branch, or law-making body, was the legislature, consisting of a house of representatives and a senate. House members were to serve two-year terms, senators four-year terms. The judicial branch was to be made up of a supreme court, district courts, county courts, and municipal courts.

Oklahoma's constitution was called a reform constitution, because it contained many new ideas which were to return democracy to the people. The constitution included initiative and referendum. By initiative, citizens could propose laws. By referendum, the citizens could vote on laws submitted to them by the legislature. In this way the people could have a direct voice in law-making.

Social reforms included the eight-hour work day in the mines and on public works. Child labor was forbidden. Prohibition, which

121. Charles N. Haskell, Oklahoma's first governor.

186

banned the sale of alcoholic beverages, was included.

The Statehood Proclamation—Oklahoma leaders set an election in the Twin Territories for September 17, 1907. The people were to vote on the constitution and on candidates for public office. Officials winning election would not take office until Congress approved the constitution and Oklahoma was admitted to the Union. Candidates for governor included Charles N. Haskell, the Democratic candidate, and Frank Frantz, the Republican candidate. Haskell won the first governor's election, and Democrats won most of the state offices and the most seats in the state legislature.

The Oklahoma constitution was sent to Washington, D.C. After some study, Congress approved it. On November 16, 1907, President Theodore Roosevelt signed the Oklahoma statehood proclamation. Officials in Washington telegraphed the news to Guthrie. A vast crowd had gathered there to celebrate Oklahoma's admission to the Union. On the same day, Charles N. Haskell was installed as Oklahoma's first governor.

CHAPTER NINE

The Sooner State

In 1907, Oklahoma's population was about 1,500,000. Governor Charles N. Haskell had the duty of launching the new state government. The foundations for state government had been formed during the territorial period. This made his task easier. Yet, he had much to do in order to fulfill the requirements for state government set forth in the constitution.

The first legislature was the busiest lawmaking body in Oklahoma history. It had to expand the state court system, establish a public school system, and adopt civil and criminal laws. In addition, it had to establish a system of taxation for raising revenue to support the state government.

Through the years the needs of Oklahomans have changed, and Oklahoma state government has changed to meet the new needs. In the 1970's, Oklahoma legislatures adopted new laws to promote the public welfare. Always, the work of the first Oklahoma legislature has served as the base upon which state leaders have made changes.

OKLAHOMA'S STATE GOVERNMENT

Oklahoma state government has served the needs and promoted the welfare of Oklahomans. The executive, legislative, and judicial offices have been filled by elected officials who have performed the duties of their offices. They have provided leadership for the

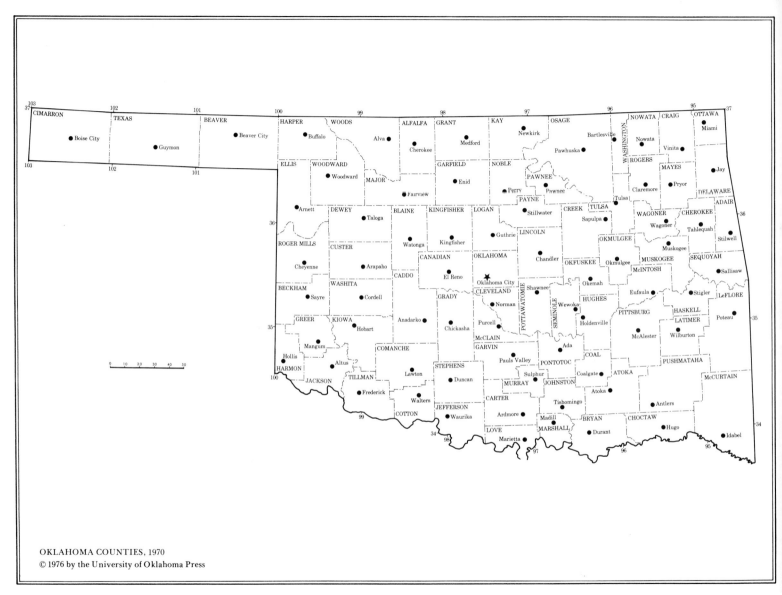

OKLAHOMA COUNTIES, 1970

© 1976 by the University of Oklahoma Press

Oklahoma Counties, 1970

state, and many state leaders have served the nation as United States congressmen and senators. Oklahoma leaders have been elected to public office through the efforts of political parties.

Oklahoma's One-Party System—Several parties have been active in Oklahoma politics since statehood. The most important political parties have been the Democratic, Republican, and Socialist parties. Until the 1960's the Democratic party won most Oklahoma elections. Thus Oklahoma was known as a one-party state. For example, every governor until 1962 was from the Democratic party. Other state officials and most of the United States congressmen and senators from Oklahoma also have been Democratic.

In recent times, Republican party candidates have been more successful in Oklahoma elections. Since 1962 the Republican party has elected two governors. And Republicans have won other state and national offices, so that Oklahoma politics seem to be moving in the direction of a two-party system.

Oklahoma Political Leaders—Some Oklahoma politicians have been such strong leaders that they have provided leadership for both the state and the nation. Oklahoma's first two United States senators were Robert L. Owen and Thomas P. Gore. Their service in the United States Senate drew favorable notice to the new state of Oklahoma. Owen, from Muskogee, was of Cherokee descent and had a keen knowledge of banking. Senator Owen drafted several important federal laws, which included the law establishing the Federal Reserve System. Gore, from Lawton, was blind. Yet he was a brilliant public speaker and an expert on foreign affairs. Robert S. Kerr was another Oklahoman serving in the United States Senate who became a national leader. During the 1950's, Kerr was called "the uncrowned king of the Senate."

Oklahoma's most important leader in national affairs was Congressman Carl Albert. During the 1960's and 1970's he served as speaker of the United States House of Representatives. This placed him in the third most important position in the national government, just below the president and the vice-president of the United States.

Many Oklahomans have been appointed to positions in the national government. The

122. Robert L. Owen, one of Oklahoma's first United States senators.

123. Thomas P. Gore, one of Oklahoma's first United States senators.

124. Robert S. Kerr, notable Oklahoma political leader.

125. Carl Albert, Oklahoma congressman who became speaker of the United States House of Representatives.

Oklahoman who held the highest executive office was Patrick J. Hurley, an attorney from Tulsa. Hurley served as secretary of war during the administration of President Herbert Hoover.

Several Oklahoma governors have provided outstanding leadership for the state. Oklahoma's first governor, Charles N. Haskell, was a daring and creative leader who proposed several important laws. One was the Bank Guaranty Law, which insured bank deposits and strengthened Oklahoma banking. The Oklahoma Bank Guaranty Law became the model for the Federal Deposit Insurance Law later adopted by Congress.

Haskell's daring was shown when he moved the capital from Guthrie to Oklahoma City. The Oklahoma Enabling Act required that the state capital be at Guthrie. Haskell was a Democrat and Guthrie was a center of Republican strength, therefore he wanted to move the center of state government. The legislature submitted to the voters a proposal to relocate the capital. In a referendum, the voters favored Oklahoma City, and on the night of the election, Haskell moved the capital to Oklahoma City.

Governor William H. Murray also ranks among Oklahoma's strongest political leaders. Murray was a colorful person and an authority on constitutional law. He had served as president of the Oklahoma constitutional convention. Murray was governor during the period of the Great Depression. His strong leadership eased some of the economic suffering in Oklahoma.

Oklahoma politics have been troubled. There has been much dispute between governors and the legislature over what is best for the state. The legislature has generally dominated Oklahoma state government. The Oklahoma constitution grants to the legislature the power of impeachment. Impeachment is the process for removing officials in the executive and judicial branches of government. The legislature has removed several executive and judicial officers by impeachment. The most important impeachment trials were held in 1923 and 1929. They resulted in the removal from office of Governor Jack Walton and Governor Henry Johnston.

When the legislature removes a governor from office, the lieutenant governor succeeds to the office of governor. After Walton was

192

impeached and removed from office in 1923, Lieutenant Governor Martin E. Trapp became governor. In 1929, when the legislature impeached and removed from office Governor Johnston, Lieutenant Governor William J. Holloway became governor.

The governors and their terms of office for the period 1907 to 1977 have been Charles N. Haskell (1907–11), Lee Cruce (1911–15), Robert L. Williams (1915–19), James B. Robertson (1919–23), Jack Walton (1923), Martin E. Trapp (1923–27), Henry Johnston (1927–29), William J. Holloway (1929–31), William H. Murray (1931–35), Ernest W. Marland (1935–39), Leon Phillips (1939–43), Robert S. Kerr (1943–47), Roy J. Turner (1947–51), Johnston Murray (1951–55), Raymond Gary (1955–59), J. Howard Edmondson (1959–63), George Nigh (1963), Henry Bellmon (1963–67), Dewey Bartlett (1967–71), David Hall (1971–75), and David L. Boren (1975–).

Political Status of Women—Until recent times, Oklahoma state government has limited the political rights of women. Women were not permitted to vote in Oklahoma elections until 1918 when Oklahoma voters approved a

126.   State Representative Cleta Deatherage.

193

127.   State Representative Hannah Adkins.

128.   Mayor Patience Latting, Oklahoma City.

constitutional amendment to permit female suffrage.

During the Phillips administration the legislature proposed a constitutional amendment which made women eligible for public office, including governor. The amendment was defeated in 1940, but two years later the voters approved it. In 1952, Oklahoma voters approved women serving on juries. Since 1950 women have become active in Oklahoma politics. Women have been candidates for several major state offices, including the office of governor, and some women candidates have won election to the Oklahoma legislature.

Political Status of Blacks—Many Oklahoma leaders were from the South, and they copied the methods used in the South to restrict blacks after the Civil War. The first legislature adopted what is called "Jim Crow" laws for Oklahoma. Before the 1950's, federal laws and court decisions permitted states to separate white and black citizens. The Oklahoma Jim Crow laws required separation of white and black races in public places. This included separate railway cars and waiting rooms, and separate toilet facilities and drinking fountains. These segregation laws also required separate schools for white and black students.

Many southern states had adopted a constitutional amendment called the Grandfather Clause. It denied voting rights to most blacks. In 1908, Oklahoma voters approved a Grandfather Clause proposal. Black leaders objected, and in 1915, in the *Guinn* case, the United States Supreme Court declared the Oklahoma Grandfather Clause unconstitutional.

Through the years blacks worked to obtain equal rights. Their progress was slow. They tried to remove segregation in education. Black students had to attend separate schools from elementary level through college. The Oklahoma black college was Langston University. Desegregation in Oklahoma education began during the late 1940's. Ada Lois Sipuel, a graduate of Langston University, applied in 1946 for admission to the University of Oklahoma School of Law. State law required University officials to deny her admission. Her attorneys appealed to the United States Supreme Court. In 1949 the court ruled that Oklahoma must provide the same instruction for black students as that given to white students.

Other black students applied for admission to Oklahoma colleges and universities. By 1950, blacks were admitted to Oklahoma colleges and universities on an equal basis. Elementary and secondary public schools in Oklahoma were desegregated after 1954. Governor Raymond Gary abolished other forms of Jim Crow law segregation such as separate rest rooms, drinking fountains, and parks.

Blacks gained equal opportunity in education. Their social status improved. More black citizens registered to vote, and they elected blacks to the state legislature, which gave them a voice in law-making. Blacks also were granted equal treatment in employment and housing.

Highlights of Action in State Government— From the thousands of laws adopted by the Oklahoma legislature after 1907, several stand out. They are notable because of their effect on Oklahoma citizens. One of the most important steps taken by the legislature was to create the Oklahoma system of education. The first legislature adopted laws forming a system of free public schools. The state board of education was created to manage the pub-

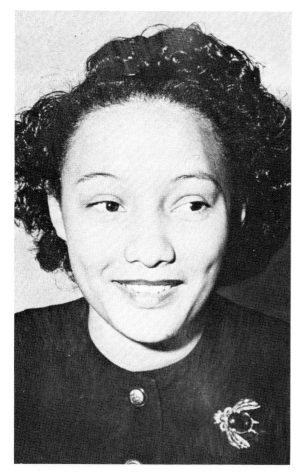

129. Ada Lois Sipuel entering the University of Oklahoma School of Law, June, 1949.

196

lic schools. State law required all Oklahoma students between the ages of eight and sixteen to attend school. In the early years, terms of school ranged from three months in some districts to nine months in others. The length of the school term was determined by the ability of the school district to support a school. Later the legislature adopted laws which equalized school financing and permitted a nine-month term for all schools.

The quality of Oklahoma education has gradually improved. Much of the state income from taxes goes for the support of the Oklahoma educational system. The Oklahoma system of higher education began in 1890, when the first territorial legislature created the University of Oklahoma, the Oklahoma Agricultural and Mechanical College, and the Oklahoma Normal School. The legislature has expanded the system of college and university education in Oklahoma, so that today there are more than thirty public-supported colleges and universities. In addition, there are several private elementary, secondary, and higher education institutions in Oklahoma.

Laws having a direct bearing on most Ok-lahoma citizens are the tax laws, which produce the revenue which supports state government. Oklahoma was one of the first states to adopt a graduated income tax. Other important sources of state income include the gross production tax on petroleum production and the sales tax. Most of the sales tax income goes to pay for social welfare programs. A tax for supporting local government and schools is the real property tax. This tax is collected by the Oklahoma counties.

One of the most important proposals drafted by the legislature was the budget balancing amendment, which was adopted during the Phillips administration. The budget balancing amendment requires that the legislature appropriate no more than the amount of tax revenue the state receives each year.

Improving state highways has been a long-time concern of the legislature. Beginning in the late 1940's, the legislature authorized the construction of modern four-lane toll roads. The Turner Turnpike connecting Oklahoma City and Tulsa was the first of several toll roads completed. The Oklahoma highway system was greatly benefited in 1956, when Congress passed the Federal Aid Highway

197

Act. This law created the national interstate highway system. Oklahoma's share of the interstate highway system includes Interstate 35, a north-south road, and Interstate 40, an east-west road.

Until 1959, Oklahoma was a "dry" state, which means that the sale of intoxicating beverages was unlawful. In that year voters repealed the prohibition amendment. This action made it legal to sell intoxicating beverages in Oklahoma.

OKLAHOMA'S ECONOMY

During the pioneer period most Oklahomans lived in the country on farms. Oklahoma towns were small. They were marketing centers for grain, cotton, and livestock. Early-day Oklahoma towns also supplied farmers with seed, tools, implements, and other farm and ranch needs. Soon after statehood, mining, oil production and refining, and lumbering became important industries.

Before 1945 there was very little manufacturing in Oklahoma. Since then, great changes have occurred in the Oklahoma economy. Several new industries have been established. Many Oklahomans have moved from farms to the cities, where they are employed in the new industries.

Agriculture—Down to 1941 the basic crops raised on Oklahoma farms were cotton, corn, and wheat. Cotton was the most important crop. Oklahoma farmers each year produced about 400,000 bales of cotton valued at over $75,000,000. Since World War II, wheat has replaced cotton as Oklahoma's leading cash crop. Each year Oklahoma farms produce about 120,000,000 bushels of wheat valued at over $300,000,000. Wheat is also Oklahoma's most important export. Nearly half of the annual wheat production is sent to foreign countries.

In western Oklahoma, broomcorn and peanuts are important crops. Most of western Oklahoma farm land is irrigated. Water for irrigation is drawn from reservoirs and deep wells. Many Oklahoma farmers use their land to produce livestock feed crops such as alfalfa, grain sorghums, and bermuda. The annual value of Oklahoma agricultural products is over one billion dollars. This is more than the value of oil production and all other industries except manufacturing.

130. Street scene in Wirt, Oklahoma, about 1920.

131.   Picking cotton in Oklahoma.

132.   Cotton auction on Main Street, Guthrie, 1893.

133.   Sorghum mill, Indian Territory.

134.   Combines harvesting a bumper wheat crop in Oklahoma.

135.   Elevator for storing Oklahoma grain, Garfield County.

Livestock Industry—From earliest times, stock raising has been an important Oklahoma industry. The Five Civilized Tribes brought horses, cattle, mules, hogs, and poultry to Oklahoma. The Plains tribes, also, were expert horse breeders. After the Civil War there were many large ranches in Oklahoma. Homesteaders broke up the big ranches, although stock raising continued to be an important industry.

Today all types of livestock are produced on Oklahoma ranches and farms. Cattle, sheep, hogs, and horses are widely raised. Beef cattle are the most numerous. Dairy farming and poultry raising are important.

Cattle production in Oklahoma is increasing. Each year Oklahoma ranch and farm herds produce nearly 2,000,000 calves. About half of the calf production is sold to stockmen in other states. However, more calves are placed in Oklahoma feed lots each year. During 1974, half a million calves were in Oklahoma feed lots.

Stock marketing facilities are found in every part of the state. One of the largest livestock markets in the Southwest is the Oklahoma City Stockyards. Since 1910 nearly 100,000,000 head of livestock have passed through this market.

Oklahoma's labor force during the 1970's consists of over 1,000,000 workers. More workers are engaged in agriculture and stock raising-related industries than any other business. An estimated 200,000 persons are employed in meat and dairy processing, canning and freezing dairy products, and grain milling.

Mining—Oklahoma is rich in mineral resources. Several Oklahoma minerals are mined and smelted for industrial use. Lead and zinc have been mined in Ottawa County in the northeastern portion of the state. This area is called the Tri-State District. At one time it was the richest lead and zinc region in the world. Between 1900 and 1950 a billion dollars worth of lead and zinc ores were mined in the Tri-State District.

Oklahoma coal is mined for industrial use. Steel mills in Oklahoma and Texas use great quantities of Oklahoma coal each year. Oklahoma coal also is marketed in Canada, Mexico, and Japan.

Other Oklahoma mineral industries include salt and gypsum production. Gypsum is used

136.   Cattle of early-day ranchers.

138.   Webber Mine, Ottawa County, part of the Tri-State Lead and Zinc Mining District.

137.   Hereford cattle on Oklahoma's western range.

139.   Coal miners near Hartshorne, Choctaw nation.

140.   Mining lead and zinc near Century, Indian Territory.

141. Arbuckle Mountains quarry producing building stone.

for several industrial purposes, including the manufacture of wallboard. Quarries across Oklahoma produce crushed rock for concrete mix and building stone. Crushed limestone is used for fertilizer and road fill. Red granite, quarried in southwestern Oklahoma, is widely used for monuments and public building construction. Oklahoma cement supports construction and highway building. Sand is used as a mix for concrete in construction and for making glass. Oklahoma clays are converted to brick and ceramic objects.

The Petroleum Industry—Oklahoma perhaps is known best as a leading producer of petroleum. The first commercial oil well was opened at Bartlesville in 1897. The famous Red Fork field near Tulsa was discovered in 1901. In 1905 drillers brought in the Glenn Pool near Tulsa. Soon Tulsa was being called "the Oil Capital of the World." By statehood in 1907, Oklahoma wells were producing over 40,000,-000 barrels of oil a year.

There was an increased demand for petroleum products because of the wide use of automobiles. This led to expansion of the oil industry, and Oklahoma had become the nation's leading producer of oil by 1920. In recent times, Oklahoma ranks among the top three oil producing states.

One of the world's richest oil fields was discovered in 1928 in Oklahoma City. Since its opening, the Oklahoma City field has produced nearly a billion barrels of crude oil. Development of rich oil fields in the Osage nation and at Cushing, Ardmore, Healdton, Tonkawa, and Seminole added to Oklahoma's petroleum production. Drillers have explored every portion of the state and nearly every Oklahoma county has yielded some oil and natural gas production.

The petroleum business is one of Oklahoma's basic industries. It employs over 100,000 workers. Oklahoma has fourteen refineries. They process nearly half a million barrels of crude oil daily. The gross production tax on petroleum is an important source of state revenue. The petroleum industry has led to the rise of many Oklahoma towns. Oil boom towns have grown up near each new field, and several of the largest Oklahoma towns began as boom towns following an oil discovery.

Lumbering—Lumbering is an old Oklahoma industry. Water-powered sawmills were in-

211

142.   Early-day oil field equipment, Creek nation field.

143.   Arkansas River steamer advertises the Oklahoma oil fields.

144. Wooden
derricks
in Oklahoma
oil field.

145. Oil derricks
and pumps
in the
Elk Basin
oil field.

stalled in Indian Territory about 1830. Before the Civil War, several steam-powered sawmills were operating in the forests of the Cherokee, Creek, Choctaw, Seminole, and Chickasaw nations.

Most Oklahoma lumbering is concentrated in the eastern part of the state. There thick forests of soft woods (pine) and hardwoods (oak, hickory, pecan, ash, and walnut) are found. Each year Oklahoma lumber companies produce over $100,000,000 worth of wood products and employ over 6,000 workers. Oklahoma sawmills turn out construction lumber, bridge timbers, fence posts, telephone poles, pulpwood for making paper, fiberboard, charcoal, and wood for furniture manufacture.

Manufacturing—State leaders have attracted manufacturing plants to Oklahoma. In 1900, Oklahoma had 500 manufacturing plants employing 2,600 workers. The annual production was valued at $2,700,000. The number of workers in industry had increased to 30,000 in 1929, with a production value of $150,000,-000. Early Oklahoma manufacturing consisted largely of meat packing and food processing, brewing, refining petroleum products, glass making, and smelting metals.

After World War II, Oklahoma manufacturing increased. By 1952, manufacturing employed 78,000 workers. The annual production value was nearly half a billion dollars. During the 1960's Oklahoma manufacturing exceeded one billion dollars in value and employed over 100,000 workers. By 1975 the number of industrial jobs in Oklahoma was 150,000. The annual value of Oklahoma industrial production presently amounts to about two billion dollars.

Oklahoma's Service Industries—Oklahoma has a varied landscape. It has mountains, forests, prairies, and plains. Many clear, sparkling streams are in the eastern portion of the state. These features make Oklahoma an attractive tourist center. Huge lakes, including Tenkiller, Grand, Gibson, Eufaula, and Texoma, are popular centers for fishing and water sports. Chickasaw National Recreation Area, which includes former Platt National Park at Sulphur, and several state parks add to Oklahoma's natural attractions. An extensive state lodge system, including Arrowhead and Fountainhead on Lake Eufaula, appeal to visitors.

In recent times tourism has become an im-

146.   Steam sawmill in the Indian Territory pine forests.

147.   Lumbering in southeastern Oklahoma in the 1970's.

148.   Early-day brick making near Guthrie, Oklahoma Territory, 1896.

149.   Coleman Harness and Saddle Shop, an early Oklahoma industry in Norman, Oklahoma Territory.

portant part of the Oklahoma economy. More than 25,000,000 people visit Oklahoma each year. The state tourist industry nets about $225,000,000. Tourism is called a service industry.

There are other important service industries in Oklahoma. They provide income for the state, support other industries, and employ many Oklahomans. About 200,000 Oklahomans are employed by local, state, and federal facilities in the state. Over 50,000 Oklahomans work at army and air force bases, the Federal Aviation Agency in Oklahoma City, and other federal installations across Oklahoma.

Oklahoma's transportation system is another service industry. Railroads were the principal carriers of people and freight in the early years of statehood. After 1941, Oklahomans shifted to the automobile for travel. Most Ok-

150. Lake Tenkiller, ideal for fishing and water sports.

151.   Fountainhead Lodge, Fountainhead State Park on Lake Eufaula.

152.   Wichita Wildlife Refuge attracts many visitors.

153. Jet plane maintenance at American Airlines, Tulsa.

154. Tinker Air Force Base, Oklahoma City.

lahoma railroads now carry freight. The one railroad passenger carrier serving Oklahoma is the Santa Fe, which is a part of the Amtrak system. It crosses the central part of the state on the run from Chicago to Houston. With improved highways, motor truck transports move much of the grain, oil, cattle, and other Oklahoma products to market. Trucks also distribute manufactured goods to Oklahoma towns. Passenger busses provide service throughout the state, including some express schedules on the Interstate highways.

Oklahomans have access to the nation and the world through air travel. Several national air lines use terminals at Oklahoma City and Tulsa. They transport passengers and freight across the nation and to many points beyond the continental limits.

Oklahoma's transportation resources were expanded in 1971 with the completion of the Arkansas River navigation project. The terminal port is situated at Catoosa, near Tulsa. Grain, oil, and other products now move to markets by barge transport.

Oklahoma's economy supports its citizens and state and local government. Oklahoma's expanding income has provided the funds to support artistic and cultural activities. These activities are important for living the quality life. Interest of its people in the arts shows that the young state of Oklahoma is achieving maturity.

CHAPTER TEN

Oklahoma Today

Oklahoma is one of the youngest states. Yet it has made great progress since 1907. Oklahoma was born in a century of rapid change. Even greater change has taken place since the end of World War II in 1945. Oklahomans have adapted to these changes.

Until recently, most Oklahomans lived on farms in the country. Since 1946, many Oklahomans have moved to the state's towns and cities. Today about three-fourths of the Oklahoma population lives in towns and cities. Only about 25 per cent of the Oklahoma population is rural.

OKLAHOMA'S POPULATION AND CULTURE

When Oklahoma was admitted to the Union in 1907, its population numbered about 1,500,-000. Oklahomans came from many different social and economic backgrounds. They also came from different religious and ethnic backgrounds. No state entered the Union with greater racial and cultural variety than Oklahoma. Before it became a territory, Oklahoma's population consisted mainly of Indians and blacks. During the territorial period they were joined by people from all states of the Union and from several foreign countries. Today, Oklahoma's population numbers nearly 3,000,000. It has doubled since statehood.

Oklahoma's Ethnic Mix—The original population was Indian. During the nineteenth century, the federal government used Oklahoma

155. Jim Thorpe, Sac and Fox Indian from Oklahoma, Decathlon winner in the 1912 Olympic Games and called the world's greatest athlete.

as the Indian Territory. It resettled over sixty tribes from other states in Oklahoma. Today Oklahoma has the largest Indian population of any state. Indians number over 100,000 in the state's population. The rich cultural heritage of Oklahoma's Indians makes it a more interesting state.

Indians were Oklahoma's earliest pioneers. They helped to tame the wilderness. Indians introduced agriculture and stock raising. The Five Civilized Tribes brought constitutional government and education to Oklahoma. After statehood, the Indian tribes furnished many leaders for Oklahoma. Indians have contributed to Oklahoma's literary and artistic advance.

Blacks are an important part of the Oklahoma population. They number about 10 per cent of the state's people. Blacks were among the earliest Oklahoma settlers. They came to Oklahoma over the Trail of Tears as slaves of the Creeks, Choctaws, Cherokees, Seminoles, and Chickasaws. Black slaves were important in opening the Indian Territory wilderness. They built roads, cleared land for farms and plantations, and labored in the fields.

156. Beavers Bend State Park, in southeastern Oklahoma.

157.   Robbers Cave State Park, southeastern Oklahoma.

158. Turner Falls, on Honey Creek in Murray County.

Blacks became free after the Civil War. During territorial times the former slaves of the Five Civilized Tribes worked on the railroads, in the mines, and on the farms and ranches. After the Civil War, the United States Army enlisted black troops. The black soldiers were stationed at the Oklahoma forts. Called "buffalo soldiers," black cavalrymen helped conquer the Plains Indian tribes.

Blacks from the South homesteaded in Oklahoma Territory and established several communities. Their best-known town in Oklahoma Territory was Langston. Blacks were segregated by Oklahoma law. Black leaders worked to remove restrictions on voting, separate schools for their children, and other forms of segregation. In recent times they have succeeded. United States Supreme Court decisions and federal laws have assisted them. They have gained equality of opportunity. Blacks have made progress in the trades, professions, and the arts.

159. Downtown Tulsa, Oklahoma.

160. Municipal rose gardens, Tulsa, Oklahoma.

161. Oklahoma City, night view.

The white population of Oklahoma came from all sections of the United States and from several foreign countries. Most settlers in eastern Oklahoma were from Missouri, Arkansas, Alabama, Mississippi, Louisiana, and Texas. In the western half of the state, many settlers came from Kansas, Nebraska, and the states of the North and East. Many Texans came to Oklahoma Territory. German and Czech communities are scattered across the state. Russian, Scottish, Polish, Welsh, Italian, and Greek settlements are situated in the mining areas of old Indian Territory.

Oklahoma's Cultural Mix—Oklahoma settlers brought with them a variety of cultures—many kinds of customs, speech, religion, and politics. The homesteader culture gradually blended with the Indian-black culture. The foreign communities further enriched Oklahoma's ethnic and cultural mix.

Oklahoma's cultural diversity is shown in the variety of religions in the state. Southern Baptists and United Methodists are the most numerous. Oklahomans also are members of the Disciples of Christ (Christian Church), Congregationalist, Presbyterian, Episcopal, Pentecostal, Church of Christ, Mennonite, Lutheran, and many other Protestant groups. The state also has Greek Orthodox, Roman Catholic, and Jewish churches. A Russian Orthodox church is at Hartshorne, a former coal-mining camp in southeastern Oklahoma.

Another important part of Oklahoma spiritual life is Indian religion. Many Indians follow the native religion. They observe the Sun Dance, Ghost Dance, and other religious festivals. The Native American Church is important to many Oklahoma Indians.

OKLAHOMA AND THE ARTS

Oklahoma is a young state, but its people have shown a strong interest in the arts. Many Oklahomans—red, black, and white—have contributed to the state's artistic and literary progress. Some of the arts in Oklahoma are very old. Interest in poetry, drama, and painting did not begin with the coming of the homesteaders in 1889. Long ago, Oklahoma Indians were creating art in many forms.

Indians and the Arts—Prehistoric Oklahomans sketched animal figures on the walls of their

235

162. "Trail of Tears" drama near Tahlequah, Oklahoma.

cave and ledge homes. Paleo-Indian artists decorated conch shells and pottery. Weavers created cloth with colorful design. Spiro Indian sculptors carved figures in stone and clay. Indians used reed flutes, skin drums, and terrapin shell rattles for musical instruments. The tribes performed a variety of dances. Indian dancing continues to be a popular form of Oklahoma culture.

The many Indian tribes resettled in Oklahoma added to the variety of native art, music, and the dance. The most important Indian invention was made by Sequoyah. He created a system of writing for his people, and Cherokees in Oklahoma used this written language. Printing presses published newspapers and books using the Cherokee alphabet.

---

163. Indian dancer at the American Indian Exposition, Anadarko, Oklahoma.

Two outstanding Indian writers were John Rollin Ridge, the Cherokee poet, and Alexander Posey, the Creek poet. Publishing books to spread knowledge and ideas is a mark of cultural advance. Well before the Civil War, books were published in Oklahoma for Indian readers. The best-known early-day publishing house was the Park Hill Press in the Cherokee nation.

Pioneers in the Arts—During the pioneer period in Oklahoma Territory, settlers labored to tame the wilderness. They worked from dawn until dark each day opening farms and establishing towns. Yet, they took a little time to meet together.

Nearly every pioneer Oklahoma community had a literary society. The members wrote poetry, short stories, and plays. They carried on debates and discussed important questions of the day.

Traveling Chautauqua groups were popular in early-day Oklahoma. The Chautauqua programs included lectures by famous speakers. Other Chautauqua entertainment consisted of plays, musical performances, and variety acts.

Modern Oklahomans and the Arts—Since statehood, Oklahomans' interest in the arts has increased. They paint and write poetry and books. Many perform as musicians. Several Oklahomans have become world-famous in the performing arts.

A number of prominent ballet performers are from Oklahoma and are of Indian descent. Yvonne Chouteau was the youngest American ballerina ever accepted for the Ballet Russe de Monte Carlo. At one time Maria Tallchief was the ranking ballerina in the United States. Other famous Oklahoma performers include Marjorie Tallchief of the Paris Ballet Company, Rozella Hightower, and Moscelyne Larkin.

The Indian dance is popular. Indian dancing provides unity for over sixty tribes living in Oklahoma. Many tribes hold powwows during the summer and autumn months. Indian dancing is a part of each program. The annual Indian Exposition at Anadarko has attracted worldwide interest for its Indian dancing.

Oklahoma artists have won wide acclaim. Indian art was popularized by Dr. Oscar Jacobson at the University of Oklahoma. During

164. Opera performance, Tulsa.

165. Augusta Metcalfe, Oklahoma artist, photographed by Paul Lefebvre.

the 1920's he established the School of Indian Art. Jacobson taught over thirty Indian artists from ten tribes. Their paintings have been exhibited throughout the United States and in several European countries. Jacobson's Indian artist students included five young Kiowas: Stephen Mopope, Monroe Tsatoke, James Auchiah, Jack Hokeah, and Spencer Asah. They came to the University campus in 1928.

Other prominent Oklahoma Indian artists include Acee Blue Eagle, Woodrow Crumbo, Jerome Tiger, Allen Houser, Black Bear Bosin, Archie Blackowl, Carl Sweezy, and Willard Stone. Possibly the best-known of the modern Indian artists is Dick West, a Cheyenne.

Non-Indian artists from Oklahoma also have been successful. John Noble was a young pioneer in the Cherokee Outlet. Later he studied art in Paris. Noble's most popular painting was titled "The Run." It depicts the race for homesteads in Oklahoma Territory. Before 1920, two famous landscape artists from Oklahoma were Nellie Shepherd and Howell Lewis.

In recent times, Oklahoma's most popular painters have been Charles Banks Wilson and Augusta Metcalf. Wilson is best-known for his portraits of Sequoyah, Will Rogers, Jim

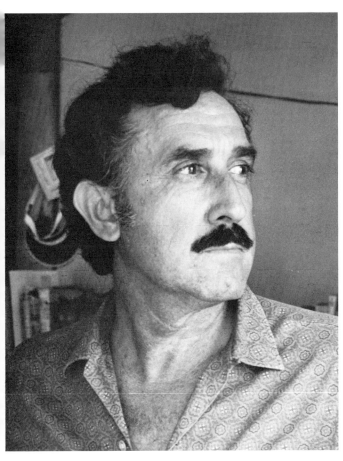

166. Charles Banks Wilson, Oklahoma artist.

Thorpe, and Senator Robert S. Kerr, and for historical murals which hang in the state capitol rotunda. Augusta Metcalf, now deceased, was a self-taught artist. She grew up in western Oklahoma during pioneer times. Her paintings are early-day scenes of the Oklahoma frontier.

Many Oklahomans have a strong interest in writing. The state has a number of writers' clubs and poetry societies which encourage authors. Several Oklahoma writers have won national fame. These include Will Rogers, George Milburn, John Oskisson, Ralph Ellison, and Lynn Riggs. Riggs's *Green Grow the Lilacs* was used as the basis for the well-known play *Oklahoma!* Rogers is most familiar as a humorist and entertainer, but he also achieved wide fame as a writer. N. Scott Momaday, a Kiowa writer, received the Pulitzer Prize in 1969 for his book *House Made of Dawn*. Oklahoma poets have received acclaim from the days of John Rollin Ridge and Alexander Posey. Prominent twentieth-century poets have included Kenneth Kaufman, George Riley Hall, Vera Holding, Melvin Tolson, and Welborn Hope.

Publishing the works of Oklahoma writers

241

is important. Many Oklahoma writers have their manuscripts published in the eastern United States. However, there are several publishers in this region. One is the University of Oklahoma Press at Norman. It produces about one hundred books a year.

OKLAHOMA'S CULTURAL RESOURCES

Oklahomans produce art, write books, and perform. Oklahomans also support the arts. Many citizens with great wealth have established art museums and galleries for the public benefit. Ernest W. Marland gave many works of art to the people of Oklahoma. These include Ponca City's Pioneer Woman Statue by Bryant Baker. Thomas Gilcrease used much of his oil wealth to collect paintings and other works of art. Later he founded the Gilcrease Institute, a fine museum at Tulsa. Philbrook Art Center, also at Tulsa, was established by Waite Phillips. Frank Phillips founded Woolaroc Museum near Bartlesville. Other art collections are situated at the Oklahoma City Art Center, the University of Oklahoma Art Museum, and the St. Gregory's Art Museum at Shawnee.

Many Oklahoma museums preserve and display the state's cultural heritage. Oklahoma's oldest museum is situated at the State Historical Society Building in Oklahoma City. Other outstanding state museums include the Museum of the Great Plains at Lawton, the Will Rogers Memorial at Claremore, Panhandle Museum at Goodwell, Pioneer Woman Museum at Ponca City, Stovall Museum at the University of Oklahoma, Black Kettle Museum at Cheyenne, Museum of the Western Prairie at Altus, and Woolaroc Museum near Bartlesville. The state's largest museum is the National Cowboy Hall of Fame and Western Heritage Center at Oklahoma City.

Oklahoma's cultural life is enriched by symphony orchestra concerts. Dramatic productions and operas are produced by local theater groups and college and university drama departments. Public libraries are in most towns of the state. Traveling libraries, the bookmobiles, deliver books to Oklahoma readers even in remote areas.

During the 1960's there was greater interest in the arts by Oklahomans than ever before. This led to the formation of the Oklahoma Arts and Humanities Council in 1967. The

167. University of Oklahoma Library.

168.   Philbrook Art Center, Tulsa, Oklahoma.

169. Will Rogers Memorial, Claremore.

council was formed to encourage the performing arts, writing, and other forms of creative expression by Oklahomans. The Oklahoma Arts and Humanities Council seeks to widen interest in and support for the arts by all citizens of the state.

OKLAHOMA'S PROMISE

During the 1970's, Oklahomans are caught up in a fast-changing world. Many changes have occurred because of advances in science and technology. Oklahomans are striving to adjust to their changing world. They seek to play a directive role in adapting new developments to useful ends. To succeed, Oklahomans need perspective. Perspective comes from knowledge and appreciation of their history. With this knowledge of their history and the perspective they gain from it, Oklahomans can better understand what is going on today. They are strengthened to face the fast-changing future with confidence and purpose. From perspective they will gain wisdom, and they will be able to direct the future. Oklahoma history is a rich storehouse from which its citizens can draw useful knowledge, understanding, and perspective.

Proper Names and Terms

Anadarko (an·a·där′kō)
Apache (a·păch′ē)
Arapaho (a·răp′a·hō)
Arbuckle (är′bŭk·al)
Arkansas (är′kan·sô)
Achiah, James (ô′chē·a)

Bemo, John (bē′mō)
Biloxi (ba·lŏk′sē)
Bogy (or Bougie), Joseph (bō′gē)
Boudinot, Elias (boo̅′da·nō, a·lī′as)

Caddo (kăd′ō)
Caddoan (ka·dō′an)
Cale (kŏ′lē)
Chautauqua (sha·tô′kwa)

Cherokee (châr′a·kē)
Cherokee Phoenix (châr′a·kē fē′nĭks)
Cheyenne (shī·ĕn′)
Chickasaw (chĭk′a·sô)
Chikaskia (shĭ·kăs′kē·a)
Chisholm (chĭz′am)
Choctaw (chŏk′tô)
Chouteau, Pierre (shō′tō, pē·âr′)
Chouteau, Yvonne (shō′tō, ē·vŏn′)
Chusto Talasah (chŭs′tō ta·lŏ′sa)
Cíbola (sē′ba·la)
Cimarron (sĭm′a·rŏn)
Coacoochee (kō·ŏ′ka·chē)
Coahuila (kō·a·wē′la)
Comanche (ka·măn′chē)
Czech (chĕk)

de Soto, Hernando   (dā sō′tō, ĕr·nŏn′dō)

Geronimo   (ją·rŏn′ą·mō)

Hokeah, Jack   (hō·kē′ą)

Ioni   (ī·ō′nĭ)

Joliet, Louis   (jō·lē·ā′, lōo′ē)

Kiamichi River   (kī·ą·mĭsh′ĭ)
Keechi   (kē′chē)
Kinnard, Motey   (kĭn′ärd, mō′tē)
Kiowa   (kī′ą·wą)

La Harpe, Bernard de   (lą härp, bąr·närd′dą)
La Salle, Robert   (lą sŏl, rŏb′ąrt)
Le Moyne, Bienville   (lą moin, byĕn′vēl)
Le Moyne, Iberville   (lą moin, ē′bąr·vēl)

Marquette, Father   (mär·kĕt′)
Micanopy   (mē·kŏn′ō·pē)
Modoc   (mō′dŏk)
Mopope, Stephen   (mō′pōp)
Moravian   (mō·rā′vĭ·ąn)
Moshulatubbee   (mōsh·ą·lăt′ą·bē)

Nacogdoches   (năk·ą·dō′chąz)
Natchitoches   (năk′ą·tŏsh)
New Echota   (ē·shō′tą)
Nez Percé (or Nez Perce)   (nā pûr·sā′ or nĕz pûrs)
Nitakechi   (nē·tą·kē′chē)

Oñate, Juan de   (ōn yăt′ā, hwŏn dā)
Onis, Luis de   (ō·nēs′, lōo·ēs′ dā)
Opothleyaholo   (ō·pŏth′lą·yą·hō·lō)
Osceola   (ŏs·ē·ō′lą)
Oto   (ō′tō)
Ottawa   (ŏt′ą·wą)
Ozark   (ō′zärk)
Ouachita   (wŏsh′ą·tô)

Parilla, Diego   (pą·rē′yą, dē·ā′gō)
Parker, Quanah   (pär′kąr, kwŏn′ą)
Pawnee   (pô·nē′)
Ponca   (pŏn′ką)
Pontotoc   (pŏn′tą·tŏk)
Potawatomi   (pŏt·ą·wŏt′ą·mē)
Poteau River   (pō′tō)

Quahada   (kwą·hŏd′ą)
Quapaw   (kwŏ′pô)
Quivira   (kē·vē′rą)

Rentiesville   (rĕnt′ēz·vĭl)

St. Denis, Juchereau de   (săn dȧ·nē′, jōō′chȧr·ō dȧ)

San Bernardo   (sŏn bȧr·när′dō)

San Teodoro   (sŏn tā·ō·dō′rō)

Satanta   (sȧ·tănt′ȧ)

Schermerhorn, John W.   (shûr′mȧr·hôrn)

Seminole   (sĕm′ȧ·nōl)

Seneca   (sĕn′ȧ·kȧ)

Sequoyah   (sĭ·kwoi′ȧ)

Shawnee   (shô·nē′)

Sipuel, Ada Lois   (sĭp′ū·ĕl)

Spiro   (spī′rō)

Tahlequah   (tŏ′lȧ·kwŏ)

Taovaya   (tŏ·ō·vŏ′yȧ)

Tawakoni   (tȧ·wŏk′ȧ·nĭ)

Tishomingo   (tĭsh·ȧ·mĭng′gō)

Tonkawa   (tŏnk′ȧ·wŏ)

Tsatoke, Monroe   (sȧ·tō′kē, mȧn·rō′)

Tullahassee   (tŭl·ȧ·hăs′ē)

Verdigris River   (vûr′dȧ·grī)

Vinita   (vȧ·nē′tȧ)

Waco   (wā′kō)

Wapanucka Institute   (wŏ·pȧ·nŭk′ȧ)

Washita River   (wŏsh′ȧ·tŏ)

Watie, Stand   (wā′tē, stănd)

Wichita   (wĭch′ȧ·tŏ)

Worcester, Samuel A.   (wŏos′tȧr)

Wyandot   (wī′ȧn·dŏt)

Definitions

abolish—To end; to do away with.

acclaim—To recognize, honor, or praise.

adaptable—Able to change under new or different conditions.

alliance—Agreement connecting two separate nations.

allotment in severalty—Assignment from tribal lands of a homestead, generally 160 acres, to an individual Indian.

ancestor—Person from whom one is descended, usually earlier than a grandparent.

archaeologist—Scientist who studies ancient remains and artifacts to recontruct the life of early peoples.

armory—Storage building for weapons.

artifact—Pottery, stone tool, or other item of material culture used by man.

artistic—Having ability to create paintings and other works of art.

auction—Public sale of land or goods by bids.

barracks—Dwelling for soldiers.

barter—To trade goods for goods rather than paying money for goods.

blockade—Closing of an enemy port by use of naval vessels.

brigadier general—Lowest of the four ranks of general.

capsize—To upturn or overturn.

cavalry—Soldiers mounted on horseback.

cholera—Epidemic disease, often fatal.

clause—Section or paragraph of a law or treaty.

Clovis man—Earliest human inhabitant of Oklahoma (15,000 years ago), identified by his slender, fluted lance point.

colonize—To establish a settlement in a new or remote land.

colony—Settlement in a new or remote land.

Columbian mammoth—Huge animal, somewhat like an elephant, once living in Oklahoma, now extinct.

constitution—Basic law of a state or nation.

culture—Beliefs, actions, and material things that make up a people's way of life.

dendrochronology—Study of rings in trees and old wood found in prehistoric sites to establish dates.

deplete—To reduce or weaken.

descendant—Child or grandchild of a person.

diversity—Difference; variation.

enabling act—Law passed by Congress making it possible for the people of a territory to write a state constitution.

environment—Physical and social surroundings.

ethnic—Having to do with racial and cultural characteristics and conditions.

evaporate—To remove moisture from; to dry.

excavate—To uncover; to dig down.

exhaust—To use up; to wear out; to end.

expedition—Journey by a group, generally explorers.

exploration—Search of a geographical region.

extinct—No longer present or living on the earth.

Folsom man—Prehistoric man, present in Oklahoma about 8,000 years ago, identified by his small, fluted lance point.

freedman—former slave who became a free person after the Civil War.

frontier—New land, unsettled and undeveloped.

geography—Study of the earth and man's use of its resources.

geology—Study of the earth and its formation.

glacier—Huge ice formation.

heritage—Inheritance; a people's past.

homestead—A farm site on the public domain, generally 160 acres.

impeachment—Process of accusing a public official of a crime or offense.

251

initiative—Process by which the people propose legislation.

irrigation—Watering of farmland from deep wells, reservoirs, or distant sources of water.

isolated—Remote; far removed.

legislature—Lawmaking body of a state or nation.

literary—Having to do with the serious writing of prose, poetry, or plays.

lottery—Process of drawing names for the distribution of land.

material culture—Things made by a people, such as tools, weapons, and houses.

maturity—Adult or fully developed stage.

migratory—Moving from one place to another.

neutral—Uncommitted; for neither side.

nonmaterial culture—Ideas, concepts, and behavior of a people, as religion, government.

obstacle—Barrier; something that stands in the way.

paleo—Early; primitive; of the Stone Age.

palisade—Log wall of a fort.

permanent—Lasting; opposite of *temporary.*

perspective—Point of view.

pirogue—Dugout riverboat.

Plainview man—Prehistoric man who lived in Oklahoma about 10,000 years ago, identified by large, slender lance point.

prehistoric age—Time before recorded history; for Oklahoma, before 1541.

pyramid—Burial structure made of stone or earth with high walls sloping upward to a point.

Reconstruction—Process by which Confederate States re-entered the Union after the Civil War.

referendum—Direct vote of the people on a law or constitutional amendment.

regiment—Unit of soldiers, before 1866 numbering about 1,500 men.

revenue—Public income from taxes.

reservation—Tract of land assigned by the federal government to an Indian tribe.

reservoir—Body of water formed by building a dam on a river or stream.

royalty—Income from oil, coal, or other mineral production.

segregate—To separate.

segregation—Separation of the races in schools and in public places and means of transportation.

suffrage—Vote; the right to vote.

syllabary—Set of written symbols for a spoken language; an alphabet.

tipi—Cone-shaped shelter of the Plains tribes, usually made of animal skins.

tourism—Promotion of touring; attraction of visitors and vacationers to a state or region.

travois—Carrier made of poles used by Plains tribes to transport household goods.

treaty—Written agreement between nations setting forth relationships and obligations.

tributary—Creek or river that flows into a larger stream or river.

turquoise—Blue or green semiprecious stone found in the Southwest.

variety—Group of unlike things.

Picture Credits

Cunningham, Robert E.: Number 85
Hurst, Wayne: Number 156
Lefebvre, Paul E.: Number 1
Library of Congress: Numbers 27, 42
National Archives (United States Signal Corps photograph): Number 22
Nye, W. S.: Number 61
Office of Media Information, University of Oklahoma: Number 129
Oklahoma City Tourism Center: Number 153
Oklahoma Historical Society: Number 59
Oklahoma Historical Society, Whipple Collection: Number 31
Oklahoma Industrial Development and Park Department: Number 141
Oklahoma Planning and Resources Board: Numbers 5, 30
Oklahoma Tourism Department: Numbers 146, 147, 148, 149, 150, 154

Philbrook Art Center: Number 41
Smithsonian Office of Anthropology, Bureau of American Ethnology Collection: Numbers 20, 64
Talkington, N. Dale: Number 161
Tulsa Chamber of Commerce: Numbers 151, 152
Western History Collections, University of Oklahoma Library: Numbers 2, 3, 4, 6, 7, 8, 9, 10, 11, 12, 13, 14, 15, 16, 17, 18, 19, 21, 23, 24, 25, 26, 29, 33, 34, 35, 36, 37, 38, 39, 40, 44, 45, 47, 49, 50, 51, 53, 54, 55, 56, 57, 58, 60, 62, 63, 65, 66, 67, 68, 69, 70, 71, 72, 73, 74, 75, 76, 77, 78, 79, 80, 81, 82, 83, 84, 86, 87, 88, 89, 90, 91, 92, 93, 94, 95, 96, 97, 98, 99, 100, 101, 102, 103, 104, 105, 106, 107, 108, 109, 110, 111, 112, 113, 114, 115, 116, 117, 118, 120, 121, 122, 123, 124, 125, 130, 131, 132, 133, 134, 135, 136, 137, 138, 139, 140, 142, 143, 144, 145, 157, 159, 160, 165
Yale University Library: Number 32

Index

255

259